Victorious Bible Curriculum

THE BEGINNING (PART 1 OF 9)

God created a home for mankind, and placed us in it to tend and guard it as His image. When we rebelled, God promised a seed of the woman to one day restore creation — and preserved that seed when our violence filled the world.

THE PATRIARCHS (PART 2 OF 9)

God chose Abraham to be the custodian of the line through which the promised redeemer would come. Abraham's grandson Jacob became the father of the twelve tribes of Israel, a nation that would bless the whole earth.

THE EXODUS (PART 3 OF 9)

For 400 years, God grew Jacob's tiny family into a nation. Through Moses, He released them from slavery to give them a new home. Despite the faithless first generation's rebellion, their children would inherit the promised land.

CONQUEST AND JUDGMENT (PART 4 OF 9)

Under Joshua, the children of the exodus conquered the promised land. After they settled in, they fell into idolatry and suffered under foreign domination. Time after time, they needed God's deliverance through a head-crushing judge.

THE KINGDOM OF ISRAEL (PART 5 OF 9)

God used Israel's first kings, the vacillating Saul and the head-crusher David, to give Israel peace. Solomon built a prosperous kingdom, which then split and fell into idolatry. After 70 years' exile in Babylon, God restored them to the land.

THE COMING OF THE MESSIAH (PART 6 OF 9)

The long wait for the serpent-crushing redeemer came to an end with the birth of Jesus of Nazareth. Raised in Galilee and baptized in the Jordan, He began to proclaim the kingdom of God and demonstrate God's love and power.

THE MINISTRY OF JESUS (PART 7 OF 9)

The blind could see, the sick were healed, the dead raised. The kingdom of God was truly at hand. But the leaders of Israel rejected the One God had sent to save them from their sins and deliver them into God's kingdom.

JESUS' FINAL DAYS (PART 8 OF 9)

On Thursday, before His arrest, Jesus ate one final meal with His disciples. Then He was arrested, beaten, falsely accused, tried, convicted and crucified. But death could not hold Him and the grave could not contain Him.

THE BEGINNING OF THE CHURCH (PART 9 OF 9)

After His resurrection, Jesus' followers received the power of the Holy Spirit to disciple the nations of the world, baptizing them and teaching them all that Jesus had said. Christ's body grew and began to crush the enemy's head under her feet.

Copyright © 2016 by Joe Anderson and Tim Nichols

All rights reserved
Printed in the United States of America
First Edition

No part of this book may be reproduced in any form or by any electronic or mechanical means, including information storage and retrieval systems, except for brief quotations in printed reviews, without the prior permission of the author.

Unless otherwise indicated, all Scripture quotations are taken from the New King James Version®. Copyright © 1982 by Thomas Nelson, Inc. Used by permission. All rights reserved.

Scripture quotations marked (NIV) are taken from the Holy Bible, New International Version®, NIV®. Copyright © 1973, 1978, 1984, 2011 by Biblica, Inc.™ Used by permission of Zondervan. All rights reserved worldwide. www.zondervan.com The "NIV" and "New International Version" are trademarks registered in the United States Patent and Trademark Office by Biblica, Inc.™

Author's translation or paraphrase indicated by an asterisk after the reference.

Illustrations by Gustave Doré
Colorized and modified by William Britton

Praise for Headwaters Bible Curriculum

These lessons are not just a way to teach the Bible to middle school kids. As I read the lessons, I found both my head and my heart irresistibly engaged. Joe and Tim have opened the grace and truth of God's Word in a way that seriously lifts us towards Christ while nudging us outward towards the world. I recommend these studies for both devotional and motivational reading!

Dave Cheadle, President of the Rocky Mountain Classis, Reformed Church of America

While I have spent quite a bit of time studying the Bible myself, I find your ideas and themes to be real food for thought and they help tie together much of the story God is telling throughout... I've already talked with people about your curriculum and have recommended they look into it for their own families. I can't loan out my copy for their perusal, because I'm using it everyday!

Linda Kidder, Home Educator, Colorado

I LOVE THIS BOOK!!!! We're just finishing up the Garden narrative. We've had such fruitful discussions—I have been pleased with it in every way. In fact, I'm hoping our church will start using it. I haven't had any problems or difficulties using the curriculum, I ONLY have good things to say about it. In fact, I'm in danger of writing in all caps I'm so enthusiastic about it.

Leah Robinson, Home Educator, Texas

I am really enjoying having this resource to work from and steer our lessons!

Christy Johnson, Bible Teacher, Bingham Academy, Ethiopia

Our family actually loves the curriculum. My children are in 5th and 8th grade and the content has suited both of their levels perfectly. To this point we hadn't found a curriculum that taught the Bible at such a detailed level that has also kept the kids engaged. We've had to slow down on the materials because otherwise they would be through them well before the school year is up. We are planning on buying the rest of the series.

Chris Turner, Home Educator, Colorado

How to Use This Book

This series of little manuals walks you through the biblical Story from end to end. Just read. Here are a few things you might want to keep in mind as you read through the Story.

- Try to love the characters. God does....
- The story is written in such a way as to make sin look stupid, but remember that the characters are all real people. No matter how stupid the choice, a real person actually looked at the options and then picked that particular one for reasons that seemed pretty good at the time. Nobody gets up in the morning and says, "I'm going to make stupid life choices that people will be mocking for centuries." Try to see it from their point of view. Ask yourself, "Why did this look like a good idea at the time?" That's how you learn to recognize temptations. It's easy to see sinful and stupid choices for what they are in hindsight, but in the moment it's often very hard. So learn to think through what these choices looked like from the inside, in the heat of the moment — you'll be amazed what you learn about yourself.
- Pay attention to the patterns. We'll point out a bunch of them as we go through the Story, but try to spot them yourself, too. If you can learn to read the Word and see the patterns in the Story, you will become able to read the world around you and see the patterns in the story God is telling right now.
- Each lesson comes with a psalm. The psalms provide us with another lens through which to look at the Story, and God has a lot to teach us that way. Sometimes we've given you an activity that will help integrate the psalm with that episode in the Story. Other times, we've just given you the psalm, and we're going to let you fill in the blanks. Read over the psalm a few times, then go into the lesson and see what comes to you. You'll be surprised what you can learn.
- As with any book that talks about Scripture, don't necessarily take our word for anything. Imagine you're sitting in a living room or around a campfire with us, and we're just talking about the Story. You're free to disagree, correct, challenge our understanding. The Word is the authority, not us — so grab your Bible and look things up yourself.

You'll find a section labeled "Activities" following the lesson. The point of this section is to immerse you as deeply in the Story as possible, through prayer, meditation on the Story, and other exercises. The "Evaluation" questions at the end of each lesson will help you to check your understanding of the material.

For Small Group Leaders
Have everyone in the group read the lesson ahead of time. Depending on how involved your group is, you can have them engage some or all of the activities, or you can save those for group time when you're together. The evaluation questions might serve as discussion starters if the conversation lags.

For Homeschoolers
Have your student read the lesson and complete the activities. (Some might be more appropriate as whole-family activities.) You can use the evaluation questions as a quiz or as discussion starters to check your student's comprehension of the lesson.

Table of Contents

Unit 8 The United Kingdom … 7
    Lesson 8.1 Yahweh Beheaded Israel and Philistia … 9
    Lesson 8.2 Israel Resurrected … 17
    Lesson 8.3 Saul Failed as King and David Anointed … 25
    Lesson 8.4 David Crushed Goliath's Head with a Small Stone … 33
    Lesson 8.5 David's Tabernacle … 41
    Lesson 8.6 Solomon's Temple … 49

Unit 9 The Divided Kingdom … 57
    Lesson 9.1 Jeroboam's Revolt … 59
    Lesson 9.2 Jehu Cleansed Israel, Yet Still Failed … 65
    Lesson 9.3 Josiah Recovered True Worship in the South … 73
    Lesson 9.4 Yahweh's Restoration of Judah … 81

UNIT 8: THE UNITED KINGDOM

An impotent old high priest, Eli, presided over Israel's worship at Shiloh, while his wicked sons did as they pleased. God prophesied through Samuel that He would kill Eli's family. God used the Philistines to fulfill the prophecy and sack Shiloh as well, effectively beheading Israel, while allowing the ark of the covenant to be captured. Using the ark as a Trojan horse, Yahweh invaded Philistia on His own, defeating the Philistines and beheading their god Dagon. The ark of Yahweh returned in triumph to Israel, coming to rest in the Gibeonite city of Kirjath Jearim.

With no high priest or central place of worship, Israel was lost, but Samuel established sacrificial worship where he lived in Ramah. In due time, Samuel gathered the people and routed the Philistine armies, and the nation finally shared in God's victory. Tired of having to rely on God to fight for them, the nation called for a king, and God gave them Saul, re-heading the nation. Initially, some didn't accept Saul as king, but after his first major victory, everyone supported him. Although promising at first, Saul quickly began to falter as his fears got the better of him. He offered a sacrifice God had forbidden him to offer, tried to kill his own son, and failed to follow God's command to destroy the Amalekites, so God rejected him as king. His son Jonathan was a bold and faithful follower of God, and he supported God's choice for Saul's successor: David.

A lowly shepherd boy, David was anointed king but would not take the throne for a long time. But when David's father sent him to bring provisions to his brothers in the army, David couldn't help but act like the king God made him to be. When everyone else was afraid of Goliath, David went out and crushed his head with a rock. Then David took Goliath's head up to Jerusalem and set it up as a warning to all God's enemies. Saul hated David and tried to kill him, but God preserved him and eventually made him king. As king, David made Jerusalem his capital and installed the ark of the covenant in a tabernacle there, instituting a service of musical offerings that consciously mirrored the Levitical animal sacrifices and involved Gentiles in the worship, fulfilling in a new way Abraham's commission to be a blessing to the nations.

Still, David was not satisfied with God living in a tent while everyone else lived in a house. God responded to David's desire by promising to build David's house into an everlasting dynasty, but didn't allow David to build His temple. Instead, David gathered the materials, but Solomon built it. In Solomon's temple, regular animal sacrifices were united to the musical service David had created, and Israel joined in worshiping God together.

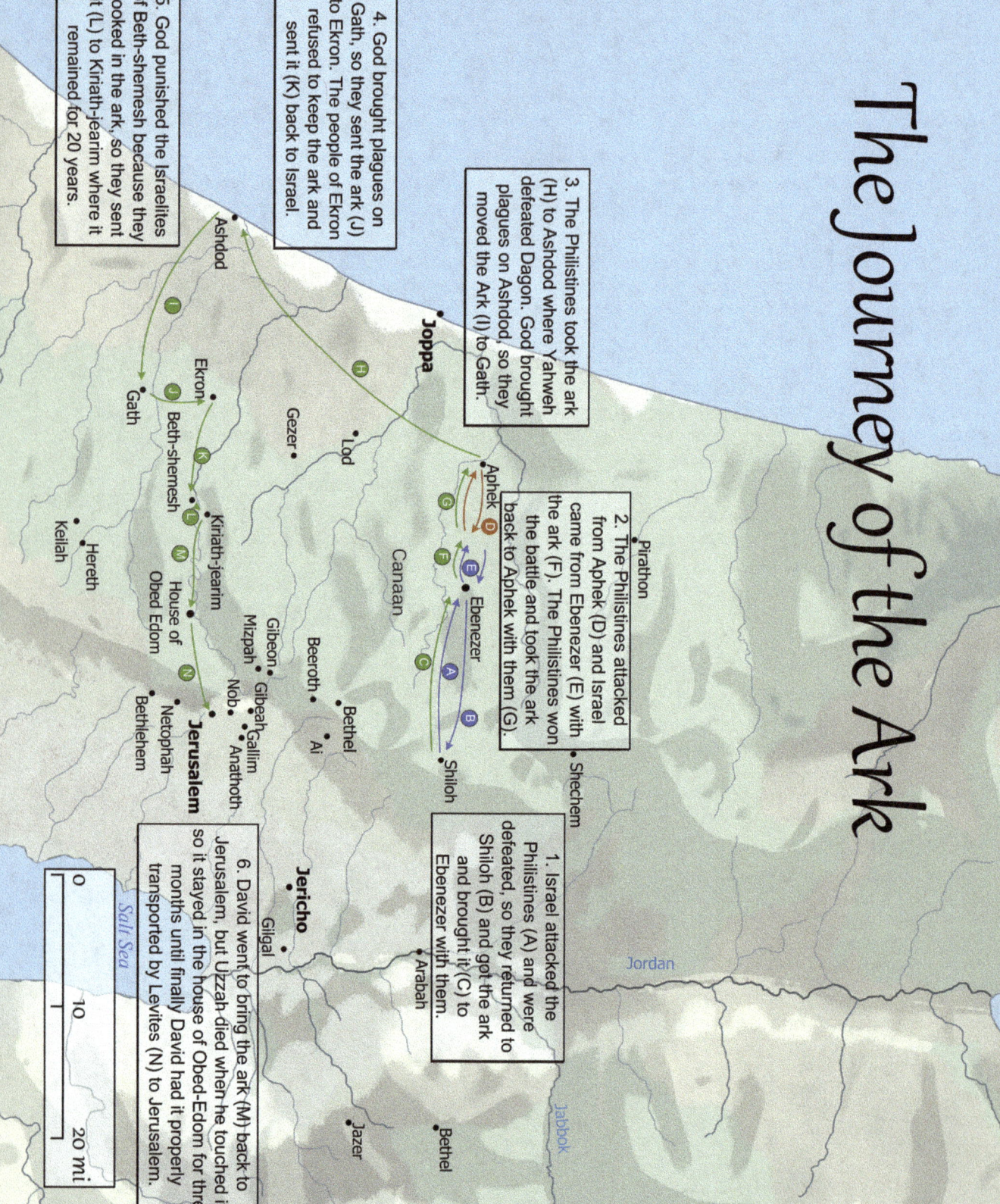

LESSON 8.1

Yahweh Beheaded Israel and Philistia

UNIT 8

THE STORY

Lesson Theme - Yahweh triumphed over both Israel and Philistia.

God had clearly said that He was going to kill Eli's wicked family, but Israel (and Eli's sons) had taken the ark out to battle. The key to this lesson is following how God resolved this situation. If Yahweh allowed Israel to be defeated, then His own reputation would suffer. But if He gave Israel the victory, He was rewarding them for treating the ark like a good luck charm. What would He do?

Samuel was of the tribe of Ephraim by birth (1 Sam 1:1), but he was apparently adopted into the family of Eli and permitted to serve in the tabernacle (1 Sam 2:18). This point will be important later in the lesson. Meanwhile, Eli's natural sons were wicked, and Eli was not able or willing to restrain them. He lectured them, but he didn't actually do anything, so they just ignored him. God sent an unnamed prophet to pronounce His curse on Eli and his whole family and then followed that up with Samuel's prophecy (1 Sam 2:27-36; 3:11-14). God further bolstered the credibility of Samuel's prophecy by his subsequent growth as a prophet (1 Sam 3:19-21). Prophecy was rare in those days (1 Sam 3:1), and Samuel was renowned as an accurate and holy representative of God, one of very few at that time.

Israel went out to battle against Philistia (1 Sam 4:1). After an initial defeat, the elders concluded (correctly) that God had not fought for them. In order to ensure that He would fight for them in

OVERVIEW

An impotent old high priest, Eli, presided over Israel's worship at Shiloh, while his wicked sons did as they pleased. God prophesied through Samuel that He would kill Eli's family, then used the Philistines to make good on the prophecy and sack Shiloh. Through the capture of the ark of the covenant, Yahweh invaded Philistia on His own, defeated the Philistines and their god Dagon, and returned in triumph to Israel, where He came to rest among Gentiles in the Gibeonite city of Kirjath Jearim.

SOURCE MATERIAL

- 1 Samuel 2-7
- 2 Samuel 6
- Joshua 9:17
- 1 Chronicles 2
- Psalm 94
- Proverbs 24:17-18

the next engagement, they brought the ark along to the battlefield (1 Sam 4:3). Bringing the ark into battle was not as crazy as it sounds. Moses had instituted a very military prayer to be said whenever the ark was moved anywhere (Num 10:35-36), and it was (correctly) understood that God Himself dwelt between the covering cherubim on the top of the ark. However, the elders misidentified how they had lost the first battle. God had not refused to fight for Israel because the ark had not gone out with the army; God had

Unit 8: The United Kingdom

OBJECTIVES

Feel...

- admiration for Yahweh's creativity in protecting His own reputation while dealing with His sinful people.
- a sense of awe at the iconic scene in the temple of Dagon.

Understand...

- that Israel was trying to compel Yahweh to save them by taking the ark to battle, but He refused to be compelled.
- that the confrontation between Yahweh and Philistia was a battle between Yahweh and the Philistine gods.
- how God gave Israel to the Philistines and still won the victory for Himself.
- that the journey of the ark followed the pattern of the exodus.

Apply this understanding by...

- considering ways in which you might be treating God like a good luck charm.

refused to fight for Israel because the nation had turned away from Him, and He was seeking an occasion to destroy Eli's family and replace them with faithful priests.

Here's the dilemma God faced: If He allowed Israel to be defeated while His very presence was with them, that made Him look like He couldn't handle the Philistines. But if He gave Israel the victory, then He was rewarding their bad behavior. What would He do?

In the short term, it looks like God's reputation was going to take a hit. God gave Israel to her enemies, they lost the battle and the ark was captured (1 Sam 4:10-11). Eli's sons were killed, and when the news came to Eli, he fell backward and broke his neck. Eli's pregnant daughter-in-law went into labor when she heard the news and named her son Ichabod ("inglorious") because the glory of God had departed from Israel (1 Sam 4:19-22). It is likely that Shiloh (Israel's place of worship) was also sacked at this time (see the prophecy in 1 Sam 2:32, and note that Samuel later instituted sacrifices elsewhere, which suggests that there was no longer a place to sacrifice in Shiloh), but no mention is made of it in the text.

God had allowed Philistia to "behead" Israel. Without a central place of worship and a functioning high priest, Israel had no real leadership at all.

The Philistines thought that they were capturing the ark. From Yahweh's perspective though, the ark was a Trojan horse—He was invading Philistia by Himself, without Israel's help. When the Philistines put the ark in the temple of Dagon (their god to whom they attributed the victory), Yahweh toppled the statue so that it was on its face before the ark (1 Sam 5:3). When they set the statue up again, Yahweh toppled it again, breaking both its head and hands off (which is to say, He crushed the head of Dagon). Meanwhile, Yahweh afflicted the city and its territories with tumors. The Philistines then sent the ark to Gath, and the people there developed tumors as well. Next, they sent it to Ekron, but by then the Philistines had figured out that they were not mightier than Yahweh. The people of Ekron refused to take it, afraid that Yahweh would kill them (1 Sam 5:11).

Realizing that they had been invaded by a hostile force mightier than they were, the Philistines

decided to send the ark back to Israel. They sent it back with offerings (five gold tumors and five gold rats). Carefully read the words of the Philistine diviners in 1 Samuel 6:2-6, and notice that they had a high regard for Yahweh, realizing that He could destroy them as He had once destroyed Egypt. God had won the battle, and He returned to Israel with the spoils of victory—and the Philistines knew it. In all this, the ark followed the pattern of the exodus: it went into captivity, Yahweh triumphed over the foreign gods, and then the ark came up into the land, bearing the treasures of the enemy.

When the ark was returned, it went first to Beth Shemesh, an Israelite city in Judah's territory (1 Sam 6:12). The Israelites there initially responded well, rejoicing and offering sacrifices and allowing the Levites to move the ark, as they should have. However, they also looked inside the ark, so God killed them (1 Sam 6:19). (Because of a difficulty in the Hebrew phrasing, translations differ on the number of dead, but for our purposes, it doesn't matter.) Afraid for their lives, the people of Beth Shemesh sent the ark up to Kirjath Jearim (1 Sam 6:21); Kirjath Jearim was not just another city, it was a *Gentile* city.

Regarding Kirjath Jearim, you have to do a little detective work to understand what was going on with this city. It was initially a Gibeonite city (Josh 9:17), and the Gibeonites were made servants of Israel. The city was apparently within the territory of Judah, because a descendant of Judah became the "father" of the city. (See 1 Chr 2—Judah's son by Tamar was Perez [verse 4], and Perez's son was Hezron [verse 5]. Hezron's son was Caleb [verse 18], and Caleb's son by his second wife, Ephrath, was Hur [verse 19]. Hur's son was Shobal who was the "father" of the city Kirjath Jearim [verse 50].) So the ark went up to a city that was under Israelite dominion, but populated with Gentiles who had been partially assimilated into Israel. This fact will be important later as we see what God did with the ark as it went up to Jerusalem: by the way He handled the ark, God made it clear that Israel's duty was to be a light to the Gentiles (see Lesson 8.5).

Psalm 94 is a plea to God to go to war with His enemies and remember His people. That is exactly what God does in this lesson—but judgment always begins in the family. God judged His own people as well, but He did it in a way that preserved them through the judgment and would ultimately grow them into maturity.

Proverbs 24:17-18 is a call to humility when God rewards you with victory over your enemies. The Philistines failed to recognize that Yahweh was in control of the outcome of the battle, and in their pride, treated the ark as if Yahweh had been vanquished. God's displeasure cost the Philistines heavily.

APPLICATION

The major application of this lesson is that God does not enjoy being treated like a good luck charm. He's a person, and He seeks a relationship with us. Israel didn't really want a relationship with Yahweh; they just wanted help with their enemies from time to time. God was unwilling to play by those rules. Only when Israel really entered back into relationship with God, led by Samuel, did God permit Israel to join in His victory over the Philistines. We often treat God like a good luck charm, just as Israel did. We only pray when we want something; and when we do pray, it's just to ask for what *we* want, instead of asking Him what He wants and seeking to know Him through understanding the situation and the Bible better.

Lesson 8.1

ACTIVITIES

1. Dagon's Defeat: Shoe-box Diorama. Possibly the single coolest scene in this whole story is the morning after the second night the ark spent in the temple of Dagon. In this iconic scene, the statue of Dagon had fallen over before the ark (bowing down before Yahweh), and its head and hands had come off. Focus on this scene. Force yourself to think through what it must really have looked like. To help yourself focus, consider making a model or shoe-box diorama of the scene to help cement it in your mind.

2. Dagon's Defeat: Improv Acting Challenge. Obviously you can't act out the scene by yourself, but consider talking some friends into helping you out. Read through the scene together, and then assign the following roles: Dagon, priests, temple maintenance workers, and worshipers. The scene will start with the Dagon character on his face before the ark. Someone will then announce that it is morning. The priests will come in and improvise a response to the scene. They will summon the maintenance workers to "fix" Dagon. The worshipers will follow quickly after. The priests can't let the worshipers in until the statue is fixed, of course, so they have to dream up something to tell the worshipers to explain why the temple isn't opening at its regularly scheduled time. Here are directions for the actors:

- Dagon: Have as much fun as possible while being "fixed." Don't make it impossible, but don't make it too easy.
- Maintenance workers: Fix Dagon.
- Priests of Dagon: Keep the worshipers from finding out what really happened. Give them a believable story instead.
- Worshipers: These priests are always lying about something. Try to find out what really happened.

3. Journal Time: Good Luck Charms. Answer the following questions.

Think of the last several prayers that you've prayed and describe what things you've prayed for below.

_____
_____
_____
_____
_____

Unit 8: The United Kingdom

Do you pray only when you need something? What are some other reasons you pray? _____
_____
_____
_____
_____
_____
_____

Do you thank God when He answers your prayers? _____
_____
_____
_____
_____
_____
_____

Are there ways you have been treating God like a good luck charm? If yes, confess this to the Lord. ___
_____
_____
_____
_____
_____
_____

God wants us to ask Him for things we need and want. But more importantly, He wants us to try to find His will in a situation; He wants a relationship with us. He doesn't want us to talk to Him only when we need something.

Lesson 8.1

EVALUATION

1. Compare the journey of the ark to Israel's exodus. _____
_____
_____
_____
_____

2. How did Yahweh protect His reputation while still judging Israel? _____
_____
_____

3. What happened to the Philistines when they captured the ark? _____
_____
_____

4. What is the significance of Dagon's head falling off? _____
_____

5. What is the significance of the death of Eli and his sons and the sack of Shiloh? _____
_____
_____
_____

LESSON 8.2

Israel Resurrected

UNIT 8

THE STORY

Lesson Theme - God restored Israel, but Israel continued to avoid a relationship with Him.
In this lesson we see how God restored His people, even when they were not perfect. Israel did not really demonstrate the kind of repentance they should have for their poor treatment of God in using the ark like a good luck charm. Israel demanded a king like all the other nations, thereby rejecting Yahweh as their ruler. But Yahweh was gracious, and He restored His people nonetheless.

The ark was in Kirjath Jearim, where it remained for a long time. Meanwhile, Samuel initiated a revival in Israel, and at his urging, the Israelites put away their foreign gods (1 Sam 7:3). Samuel gathered them for prayer, and the Philistines came up to attack. Samuel did not lead the army; he offered sacrifices and prayers, and God gave Israel the victory (1 Sam 7:10). Worship is a weapon!

God protected Israel from Philistia all the days of Samuel and established Samuel as a judge. Samuel judged Israel and rode an annual circuit between Bethel, Gilgal, and Mizpah, but lived at Ramah (1 Sam 7:15-17). There he built an altar and offered up sacrifices (it appears that Shiloh was sacked and the tabernacle worship had ceased at this time). For a time, Israel's worship was concentrated in the person of Samuel, who continued to function as a judge.

As Samuel got older and his sons grew up, he established them as judges as well, but they were

OVERVIEW

Yahweh "beheaded" Israel by allowing the Philistines to sack Shiloh and kill Eli's heirs, while attending to Eli's providential death Himself. With no functioning high priest and no central place of worship, Israel no longer had any formal leadership—no head. Shortly thereafter, Yahweh literally beheaded the Philistine god Dagon, making his statue fall down in front of the ark. Knowing that Yahweh had beaten them, the Philistines sent the ark back to Israel where it came to rest in Kirjath Jearim. Meanwhile, Samuel, the closest thing Eli had to an heir, established sacrificial worship where he lived, in Ramah. In due time, Samuel gathered the people and routed the Philistines, and the nation shared in Yahweh's victory. The nation then called for a king, and Yahweh gave them Saul, "re-heading" the nation. At first, some Israelites didn't accept Saul, but after his first major victory, the whole nation was behind him.

SOURCE MATERIAL

- 1 Samuel 7-12
- Deuteronomy 17:14-20
- Judges 11
- Psalm 90
- Ecclesiastes 10:20

17

Unit 8: The United Kingdom

OBJECTIVES

Feel...

- dissatisfied with the Israelites' lack of repentance for treating Yahweh like a good luck charm.
- joy that God restored Israel in spite of their bad behavior.
- disappointment with Israel's desire to be like all the other nations.

Understand...

- the significance of Samuel restoring sacrificial worship at Ramah: even though the tabernacle no longer functioned, Samuel was leading Israel into right relationship with Yahweh.
- that the victory over the Philistines was Yahweh's victory, and Israel got to share in it.
- that Israel's desire for a king was another way of avoiding relationship with God.
- that God honored Israel's desire by giving them what they wanted (even though it wasn't what they needed).
- that although it took some time for Saul to be accepted, his early reign was a success.

Apply this understanding by...

- identifying battles in your own life you would like for God to win so that you can share in the victory.
- identifying the God-substitutes you use in your life to avoid having to enter into relationship with God.

wicked (1 Sam 8:3), and the elders of Israel told Samuel that they would rather have a king like the other nations.

It wasn't bad in itself for Israel to want a king. The book of Deuteronomy had already set forth the laws for a king centuries earlier (Deut 17:14-20). God clearly expected them to have a king. On the face of it, now seemed like a good time. Samuel had been a great judge, but he was getting old, and his sons were not fit to take his place. Deuteronomy even says that Israel could have a king "like all the nations" (Deut 17:14) So what was the problem?

A faithful, God-fearing Israel seeking the king God wanted for them would have been fine. An idolatrous Israel, bowing down to the gods of other nations and seeking a king like the other nations, was something else entirely. Up to this point, when any foreign invader came against them, Israel had to appeal to God for help. Israel wanted a king so that they could appeal to the king for help, instead of having to go directly to God.

Samuel took Israel's desire for a king as a personal rejection of him, but God set him straight. "They have not rejected you," He told Samuel. "They have rejected me, that I should not reign over them" (1 Sam 8:7). God was exactly right, and therein lay Israel's sin.

In spite of Israel's bad intentions, God honored their request, but not right away. Instead, He instructed Samuel to give them a speech about what it would be like to have a king (1 Sam 8:9) and sent them all home.

Later, Saul, the son of a very powerful Benjamite named Kish, was out looking for some lost donkeys, but couldn't find them anywhere (1 Sam

Lesson 8.2

9:1-3). He had been searching for so many days, that he realized his father was going to stop worrying about the donkeys and start worrying about him instead. Saul was about to give up and go home when the servant travelling with him said, "Listen, there's a seer in this city, let's ask him" (1 Sam 9:6*). So they went to the city where Samuel lived.

Unbeknownst to them, God had told Samuel the day before that He was going to send a Benjamite whom Samuel should anoint as king (1 Sam 9:16). So when Saul came to the city gate, God said to Samuel, "He's the man I told you about yesterday" (1 Sam 9:17*). In God's providence, Saul approached a man at the city gate and asked for directions to Samuel's house, and the guy said, "I'm Samuel—go up to the high place for the sacrifice, eat with me, and tomorrow I will send you back and tell you everything that is in your heart. Don't worry about the donkeys—they already found them. And who does all Israel desire, if not you and your father's house?" (1 Sam 9:19-20*)

Of course, Saul balked at that last bit; but the next day, as he was sending Saul away, Samuel anointed him king of Israel, predicted a number of confirming signs, and told Saul to meet him in Gilgal in seven days (1 Sam 10:1-8). The signs that Samuel prophesied all came true, but Saul told no one what Samuel had said to him.

When the seven days were up, Samuel called all Israel together and announced that the Lord would choose a king (1 Sam 10:17). They then appeared to be casting lots—first, the tribe of Benjamin was chosen, then the appropriate clan, and eventually, Saul. But he was not there. When they looked for him, they found him hiding among the equipment and brought him out (1 Sam 10:22).

The people saw that Saul was taller and more handsome than anyone else, and they were impressed. Samuel explained the behavior of royalty to them all, and then Saul went home to Gibeah. A certain number of men went with him whom God had called to devote themselves to his service. But there were others who dissented and didn't believe Saul could reign over them (1 Sam 10:26-27).

Israel's situation remained the same until the next enemy attack. In order for the next part of the story to make sense, you have to understand that in those days, one way a king would build his kingdom was by putting people under tribute. He would go to war with a city or an area and threaten to destroy them all if they did not pay him so much gold, grain, or whatever they had. They would agree, and in return, he would usually agree to protect them against raids from other kings.

Nahash the Ammonite came up to fight against the Israelite city Jabesh Gilead. The people of Jabesh Gilead offered a peace treaty—Nahash would not attack them and they would serve him—and Nahash agreed, on the condition that he also be allowed to put out the right eye of each person in the city, in order to bring shame on Israel (1 Sam 11:1-2). Why would he do this? There was a long history of tension between Israel and Ammon. The Ammonites were sons of Ben-Ammi, son of Lot by his younger daughter. God had given them a home (Deut 2:19-21), and He insisted that Israel leave them alone. However, Ammon had not helped Israel when God brought them up out of Egypt, and Ammon had fought against Israel periodically since that time, most notably in the days of Jephthah (see Judg 11).

Unit 8: The United Kingdom

The men of Jabesh Gilead agreed to Nahash's conditions, if he would first give them seven days to see if anyone would help them (1 Sam 11:3). Nahash consented, and Jabesh Gilead sent out messengers to Israel. When the messengers came to Gibeah where Saul lived, he was out in the field with his herds. As he was coming in from the fields, he heard the weeping of all the people and asked what was going on. When Saul heard the news, the Spirit came upon him, and he was furious (1 Sam 11:6). He cut a yoke (pair) of oxen in pieces and sent the pieces out into all Israel with a message: any man who did not come out to the battle, Saul would come and cut his oxen into pieces. (Israel's was a farming culture, and oxen were both expensive and important for doing the work. It might have been a little like sending out a messenger with a piece of a crushed car today.)

Israel gathered an army of 300,000 men who marched against the Ammonites, crushing their army (1 Sam 11:11). After the battle, the people wanted to punish the rebels who had earlier rejected Saul as king, but Saul restrained them. At Samuel's leading though, the people all went to Gilgal to renew the kingdom (1 Sam 11:15). Saul was re-crowned; Samuel again instructed them to fear the Lord and honor the king He had given them.

APPLICATION

We all have a variety of problems in life, and we need to see victory over them. But the victory we need is not whatever we can cobble together from our own efforts; we need the victory that God will give us. Like the Israelites, our problems are too big for us, and we can't handle them without God's help. Like the Israelites, the path to victory leads us into worship. When we give up our idols and relate to God properly, then His victories become ours.

Also like the Israelites, we are prone to temptations even when we are doing well. Israel got right with God and triumphed over the Philistines, but then they asked God for a king so they wouldn't have to go directly to God for help in the future. Even when we are right with God, being so dependent on Him makes us nervous, and we often reach out for a substitute. What are the God-substitutes in your life? They can be good things—in fact, they often are—just as a king was a good thing that God planned to give Israel all along.

What do you look to for consolation and help when you should be looking to God? Family? Friends? Food? Entertainment? Sports or exercise? All these things are good gifts from God, and we are meant to enjoy them (1 Tim 6:17). But we are not meant to turn them into substitutes for God.

So what does it look like practically to enjoy the consolation of a good friend when things are rough, but not turn your friend into a God-substitute? There are two wrong ways to do this, and the goal is to find the road in between these two ditches.

If you talk to your friend, but you don't talk to God, you can be sure you have a problem; so first of all, *pray*. Bring the situation to God, lay it out before Him, and as best as you can, trust Him with it. If you

Lesson 8.2

really don't trust Him with it, don't lie to Him and say you do—admit that you don't think He cares, or you don't think He can do it. Tell the truth, and then see how God will direct you.

If you talk to God, but you don't talk to your friend, you have a different kind of problem. God gave us friends in order to have help and encouragement (Eccl 4:9-10). He doesn't mean for us to "only rely on God" in a way that excludes other people; that's not what God wants for us. So by all means, take advantage of the people whom God has put into your life to provide comfort. He gave them to you; He wants you to enjoy them.

The same goes for anything else. If you handle your problems with exercise, ice cream, or a movie, and don't take them to God, then you have a problem. If you're too "holy" to de-stress with God's good gifts, then you also have a problem. If you're doing both, then don't worry too much about the proportions. If something is out of balance, God will let you know.

ACTIVITIES

1. Personal Reflection and Journal Time. Israel used the ark as a good luck charm, thinking they could manipulate God to do what they wanted Him to. God ended up winning the battle against the Philistines, but on His own terms and without the help of the Israelites. When they were willing to worship Him, God allowed them to join Him in His victory over the Philistines. We face the same temptation, to use God as a good luck charm. Consider the following questions and write about it in the space provided below.

In what ways have you tried to use God as a good luck charm in your life, just like Israel did? _____
_____
_____

How did it work out for Israel when they tried to use God without worshiping Him? _____
_____
_____
_____

What happened when Israel worshiped God? _____
_____
_____
_____

Unit 8: The United Kingdom

What are some battles in your life that God wants to win, and how can you join Him in these victories?_____

_____

_____

_____

_____

2. Journal Time: Avoiding God. Any time you struggle, any time you're angry or sad or afraid, is an invitation to engage with God and seek His help. When do you typically get…

- angry (enraged, upset, frustrated, irritated)?
- sad (depressed, heavy-hearted, down)?
- afraid (concerned, worried, fearful)?

List one typical situation for each of these three emotions. Then write down what you usually do when you're in that situation. Do you move toward God or away from Him? How can you begin to move toward God in these situations, if you don't already?

Angry:_____

_____

_____

_____

_____

Sad:_____

_____

_____

_____

_____

Lesson 8.2

Afraid: _____
_____
_____
_____
_____
_____
_____

EVALUATION

1. Why did Samuel start offering sacrifices at Ramah? _____
_____
_____

2. How did Israel eventually beat the Philistines? _____
_____
_____

3. What was Samuel's strategy for dealing with the Philistine threat? _____
_____
_____

4. How did Israel receive having Saul as king? _____
_____

5. How did Saul handle his first major challenge? _____
_____
_____

LESSON 8.3

Saul Failed as King and David Anointed

UNIT 8

THE STORY

Lesson Theme - The pride of Saul and the humility of David

Saul really failed as king pretty early in his reign, so much so that God rejected him. The foundation of Saul's failure was his pride which led him to sin in three ways. (1) He rebelled against God, his Father (a sin of father-hatred); (2) he threatened his army and his son—his people (a sin of brother-hatred); (3) and he failed to obey his requirement to completely destroy the Amalekites (a sin of intermarriage). He failed as a priest, king and prophet. As a result, the kingdom was taken out of Saul's hands, and David anointed in his place.

Saul's triple failure

Before we get into the details of this story, we need to do a little set-up work. In the beginning God created Adam and put him in the *garden*. The garden is said to be situated in the *land* of Eden, and outside of the land lies the *world*. Adam's sin in the garden was a sin against God as Father, a rejection of His authority and rebellion against Him: father-hatred. As a result, Adam was kicked out of the garden and lived in the land of Eden. Adam's son, Cain, committed the characteristic sin in the land by killing his brother: brother-hatred. As a result, Cain was cursed from the land and forced to be a wanderer and a vagabond in the world (Gen 4:11, 16). Further down the road, the descendants of Adam dwelling in the world disobeyed God by marrying off their daughters to those who were off limits: intermarriage (Gen 6:1-2). The sin in the world is taking that which is forbidden by God.

OVERVIEW

Saul was anointed as king and showed signs of being the real head-crusher for Israel, but not long after his reign began, he started to falter. He arrogantly disobeyed God and offered a sacrifice that God had forbidden him to offer; he threatened his own son, and he failed to completely destroy the Amalekites. He sinned in the garden, the land and the world and was rejected as king. Saul's son Jonathan was a faithful and bold follower of the Lord, but He was not God's chosen one to deliver Israel from this evil king and their surrounding enemies. God chose and anointed David, a lowly shepherd boy, to be the head-crushing deliverer of Israel.

SOURCE MATERIAL

- 1 Samuel 13-16
- Psalm 51
- Proverbs 29:25

These three spheres of life: garden, land and world and the sins associated with each of them: father-hatred, brother-hatred and intermarriage, provide a lens through which to see the entire world. All of our lives can be divided up into these three areas, and these three sins are among the chief temptations in each area. For example, as a Christian, your relationship with God is your garden; your relationship with Christians is your land; and your relationship with unbelievers is your world. You will be tempted to

25

Unit 8: The United Kingdom

OBJECTIVES

Feel...

- saddened by Saul's failures.
- thankful that God had a plan and chose a good king for Israel.

Understand...

- the meaning of the *garden, land, world* scheme.
- the characteristic sin in the garden is father-hatred; the characteristic sin in the land is brother-hatred; and the characteristic sin in the world is intermarriage.
- Saul's three sins and how they fit the *garden, land, world* scheme:
  - Father-hatred: disobedience to God's command not to sacrifice before battle
  - Brother-hatred: withholding food from his men and nearly killing his son
  - Intermarriage: failure to completely destroy the Amalekites
- that God rejected Saul because of his arrogant disobedience in these three ways.
- that, although David was not who you would expect to be king, he was the one chosen by God—which is what really matters.
- that when Samuel anointed David, the Spirit left Saul and fell on David.

Apply this understanding by...

- trusting that when God calls you to a task, you are the right person for the job even if you don't feel like you are.
- accepting that you cannot do the work God has given you unless you make room for the Spirit to work in and through you.

rebel against God as Father, hate your Christian brothers, and become like the world. Saul's life exemplified failure in all three of these areas.

Saul's first military act as king of Israel was to attack the Philistines who had long been a thorn in Israel's side. For many years, until Samson weakened them, the Philistines had controlled Israel; then Samuel finally led Israel in a decisive battle that broke the Philistines' control over them. When Saul became king, the Israelites were no longer under Philistine control, but the two nations were constantly at each other throats. Furthermore, the Philistines had made sure there were no weapons in Israel *and* no blacksmiths to make and sharpen them (1 Sam 13:19), so Israel was still at a decided tactical disadvantage.

So Saul set his men up on the edge of the Philistine territory. His army of 3,000 was split into two groups: 1,000 men went with Jonathan to the town of Gibeah, while Saul had 2,000 men a few miles away at Michmash (1 Sam 13:2). Jonathan and his men made the first move and attacked a Philistine garrison at Geba, a town between Gibeah and Michmash. Jonathan's attack provoked a huge response from the Philistines—30,000 chariots and 6,000 horsemen assembled at Michmash where Saul and his men were encamped. The men gathered with Saul became frightened, ran and hid (1 Sam 13:6).

Saul, however, went to Gilgal. Samuel had instructed Saul to wait there for seven days, at which time Samuel would come and offer the appropriate sacrifices in preparation for battle (1 Sam 13:8). By now most of Saul's army had fled, and Saul became impatient. Instead of obeying Samuel—the prophet through whom God spoke—Saul offered the sacrifices himself (1 Sam 13:9). This was Saul's first sin and, like the sin of

Adam, was a sin against God the Father, a sin of priesthood.

Saul's offering sacrifices in Samuel's place may not sound like a *big* sin. After all, the sacrifices were going to be offered by someone; Samuel was supposed to do it, but he was late. Saul was just being a good leader; the Philistines could attack at any time, and Saul wanted to be prepared before the Lord when they did. Actually, these are exactly the excuses Saul used when Samuel pointed out that his sin *was* a big deal (1 Sam 13:11-12). They sound like reasonable explanations for his behavior, but Samuel, and the Lord, didn't think so. Saul's disobedience *was* a big deal, in the same way that eating from the fruit of the tree was a big deal for Adam. Eating fruit when God said not to is a big deal, and for Saul, offering sacrifices when God told him not to was a big deal. Saul's was plain rebellion against a direct command of the Lord.

As a result of this sin, Samuel told Saul that the kingdom would be taken away from him. More specifically, Samuel told him that the Lord was looking for a man after His own heart, and that man would be the next king (1 Sam 13:14).

Samuel then left Gilgal, and Saul took the 600 men who remained with him to Gibeah and joined forces with those who were left with Jonathan (1 Sam 13:15). The Philistines were still encamped at Michmash. Gibeah and Michmash were separated by a steep crag, with tooth-like rocks on either side of the valley. Jonathan, being a young bold warrior who trusted in the Lord, crossed the craggy valley and attacked the Philistines (1 Sam 14:11-14). The Philistines quaked in fear, a fear which God matched and magnified by sending an earthquake (1 Sam 14:15). Saul took advantage of the opportunity and attacked the confused camp of the Philistines, driving them back to Beth-Haven.

At this point we come to Saul's next big sin. At some point that day, Saul had forbidden his army, under a curse of death, from eating until they defeated the Philistines (1 Sam 14:24). Saul had probably given this order when Jonathan and his armor-bearer were attacking the Philistines, because Jonathan never heard the command. It was a rash and stupid vow for Saul to make and showed little deference for his men. As the army continued to march toward the Philistines, some of whom had retreated to Aijalon, Jonathan ate some honey that he saw in the forest (1 Sam 14:27). When Saul discovered what Jonathan had done, he threatened to kill him, but the army stopped Saul and saved Jonathan (1 Sam 14:44-45).

Saul sinned here on a couple of levels. First, it was a rash vow to make—instead of providing for his army fighting an intense battle, he forbade them from eating. Second, Saul was actually willing to follow through with his rash vow and kill his own son who had not even heard the command. Bottom line is that Saul's was a sin against his own brothers, the sin of a king in the land.

In 1 Samuel 15, Samuel approached Saul with a message from the Lord, "Now go and attack Amalek, and utterly destroy all that they have, and do not spare them. But kill both man and woman, infant and nursing child, ox and sheep, camel and donkey" (1 Sam 15:3). In obedience, Saul mustered his army and attacked the Amalekites, but was unwilling to follow through on God's command to totally destroy them; his army kept the good stuff, but totally destroyed anything they didn't want to keep for themselves (1 Sam 15:9).

Unit 8: The United Kingdom

This was Saul's third sin, a sin against God in the world. Saul's third sin is analogous to the sin of the sons of Adam in Genesis 6; their sin was intermarriage with those whom they were prohibited from marrying. Saul and his men kept everything that was good—they "intermarried" with the produce of the Amalekites. This is a sin in the area of prophecy: failure to hear and obey the word of God.

As a result of these three sins, God completely rejected Saul as king—even after he repented and worshiped the Lord (though one doubts the sincerity and depth of his repentance—1 Sam 15:30-31). Following these events, Samuel never saw Saul again, and the Lord regretted that He had made Saul king over Israel (1 Sam 15:35).

David anointed as king
When Saul was selected as king, he was in some ways the obvious choice—the tallest and most handsome man in Israel. David, in contrast, was the lastborn; he wasn't tall—he was a relatively short red-head. He was handsome, but he wasn't fearsome (1 Sam 16:7, 12). But when God rejected Saul, David was the one He chose instead.

When Samuel anointed David, we read that "the Spirit of the LORD came upon David from that day forward" (1 Sam 16:13). In contrast, since Saul had been rejected by the Lord, "...the Spirit of the LORD departed from Saul, and a distressing spirit from the LORD troubled him" (1 Sam 16:14).

This is an interesting contrast, but it gets weirder. Saul was tormented by a distressing spirit and sought relief, so his attendants suggested that he call for David to play the harp for him, since the Lord was with David (1 Sam 16:15-16). So Saul took David into his service, and "so it was, whenever the spirit from God was upon Saul, that David would take a harp and play it with his hand. Then Saul would become refreshed and well, and the distressing spirit would depart from him" (1 Sam 16:23).

APPLICATION

The biggest difference between David and Saul in 1 Samuel 16 is that David had the Spirit and Saul didn't. This is the key to Christian living. Of course, the Holy Spirit indwells believers today and God will never take His Spirit from us. On the other hand, there is such a thing as a Spirit-filled Christian *and* a Christian who shows no evidence of the Spirit living in him (Eph 5:18). You cannot cause the Spirit to work in your life; the Spirit blows where He wishes, but you can make room for the Spirit and pray for His influence in your life. David witnessed what it meant to have the Spirit's presence withheld when he saw Saul being tormented by a distressing spirit. Saul sinned and the Spirit departed, but the point is *not* to live sinlessly; the point is to live honestly. David sinned greatly against the Lord, but confessed his sin and prayed for the Holy Spirit's presence in his life. Read Psalm 51 for an example of how David made room for the Spirit even when he had sinned against the Lord (especially verses 10-12).

Notice how much of a role fear played in motivating Saul to sin. He offered sacrifices because he was afraid that his army would disperse if he waited any longer. He tried to kill David because David was becoming more popular than he was (and remember that his whole appeal to Israel was based on his good looks and his early performance in killing Israel's enemies). Proverbs 29:25 is a meditation on how fear destroys people.

ACTIVITIES

1. Contrast Saul and David. Saul and David were both chosen by God and anointed as king of Israel. Contrast Saul and David in the space below. List as many differences as you can. Be sure to contrast how they were anointed, their appearance, etc., but go beyond those things to contrast their character.

Saul	David

Unit 8: The United Kingdom

2. Journal Time: David was quick to repent, and paying attention to the way David repented can teach us how to repent thoroughly. Read through the five movements of Psalm 51 and summarize each one.

Vv. 1-6 _____

_____

Vv. 7-11 _____

_____

Vv. 12-13 _____

_____

Vv. 14-17 _____

_____

Vv. 18-19 _____

_____

Measure Saul against this biblical example of godly repentance. How did Saul fall short? _____

_____

_____

Write your own psalm of repentance regarding one of your frequent sins, following the pattern David set in Psalm 51. Pay particular attention to areas where your own repentance tends to fall short of the pattern David set. _____

_____

_____

_____

_____

_____

_____

_____

Lesson 8.3

EVALUATION

1. What do the three geographical locations from the first few chapters of Genesis, *garden, land, world,* represent? _____
_____
_____
_____

2. What is the characteristic sin in the garden? _____
_____

3. What is the characteristic sin in the land? _____
_____

4. What is the characteristic sin in the world? _____
_____

5. What were Saul's three sins before he was rejected as king, and how do they relate to the garden, land, world scheme? _____
_____
_____
_____
_____
_____

6. Why did God reject Saul as king? _____
_____
_____
_____

7. What happened when God anointed David? _____
_____
_____

LESSON 8.4

David Crushed Goliath's Head with a Small Stone

UNIT 8

THE STORY

Lesson Theme - David: a humble head-crusher who trusted in the Lord

In the previous lesson, God rejected Saul and took His Spirit from him. God chose David instead and poured the Spirit out on him. Throughout this lesson, the differences between David and Saul come out in sharper contrast as we see how they dealt with the enemy of Israel. Since Saul had rebelled against God, he was unable to face the giant in humility and crush his head. David, however, defeated Goliath and proved to be a worthy king long before he gained the position.

Background

In Lesson 6.3 (in *Conquest and Judgment*), we learned how Samson knocked down the Philistine temple, killing the five kings of the Philistines. When that occurred, Israel was under the domination of the Philistines; they payed tribute to the Philistines to secure their safety. But when Samson crushed the heads of the five Philistine kings, he set the stage for finally freeing Israel from Philistine control. The Israelites were freed some years later when Samuel (a contemporary of Samson) led Israel into battle against the Philistines at Mizpah (1 Samuel 7). The Philistines remained in the land after this, and they were a formidable foe, but they didn't control Israel anymore. Occasionally the Philistines would engage Israel in battle, and they would fight for who would get to control the other. The story of David and Goliath occurred at one such battle.

OVERVIEW

David was anointed as king of Israel, but God did not place him on the throne right away. In fact, David's reign was still a ways in the future. Nevertheless, when David's father sent him to bring provisions to his brothers at a battle between Israel and Philistia, David couldn't help but act like the true head-crushing king of Israel—while Saul and his army quaked in fear. David set aside his own honor, trusted in the Lord and crushed the head of Goliath with a stone. He then took Goliath's head to Jerusalem and set it up as a warning to all of God's enemies.

SOURCE MATERIAL

- 1 Samuel 17
- Psalm 18
- Proverbs 29:25

David and Goliath

Goliath is the serpent of the story and he was dressed like it. It says in 1 Samuel 17:5 that Goliath was wearing a very heavy coat of armor; many translate this as a coat of mail, but in Hebrew it literally says he was wearing scales, like a serpent. Goliath was also a big character, at least a couple of feet taller than the average man in Israel's army. He was well-trained and physically strong.

David is the hero of the story, but not the typical hero. If anyone was in position to be the hero,

Unit 8: The United Kingdom

OBJECTIVES

Feel...

- inspired by David's boldness and God's faithfulness when David faced Goliath.
- thankful that God had rejected the weak Saul and anointed David.

Understand...

- that Goliath is the serpent of the story.
- that Saul *should have* been the hero of the story, but God had rejected him and chosen David.
- that Goliath was initiating an honor-fight, one Saul would've had a decent chance at.
- that David shed his own honor to fight for God's honor before he engaged Goliath; David was therefore mocked by Israel's army as well as by Goliath.
- that David was the underdog, but by refusing armor and choosing a long-distance weapon, he picked up some advantages in the fight.
- that when David defeated Goliath, he was honored by his own people.
- that David took Goliath's head to Jerusalem to threaten the Jebusites who lived there and stake a claim to the city he would later make his capital.
- that David probably put Goliath's head on display at Golgotha (a contraction of Goliath of Gath)—the same place where Jesus would crush the head of the serpent on the cross.

Apply this understanding by...

- being humble but bold in pursuing God's honor like David was, even if it means enduring mockery for a time.

Saul was the man. Although Goliath would have had the size advantage, Saul was a big man and a strong warrior; this would've been a real fight for honor. Had Saul stepped up, he would have worn armor and carried a spear just like Goliath; if Saul had won, his honor would have been secured and Israel saved. But of course, Saul was afraid like the rest of his people, since he had been been rejected by the Lord.

This story is often told as an underdog story. David went into the fight with multiple disadvantages and came out a victor anyway. This is sort of true; David certainly was the smaller and weaker opponent; but he had the advantage of speed without any armor to encumber him. Furthermore, Goliath was armed for close range hand-to-hand combat. His heavy spear was not meant for distance throwing, even for a man of his size. David was armed for fighting at a greater distance. A hand sling was not a toy; it was capable of hurling a tennis ball-sized stone over 100 yards at up to 60 mph. It was a serious weapon of war.

David refused to wear Saul's armor and to carry a spear in order to gain the tactical advantages of speed and distance. In doing so, he also gave up the pursuit of his personal honor. Again, this was *supposed to be* an honor fight; the challenger was supposed to face Goliath man-to-man with armor and a shield. David rejected the man-to-man fight because he wasn't interested in preserving his own honor, but the Lord's.

David was very clear about the fact that it was not him, but God, who was going to defeat Goliath. He said this both to the Israelites and his brothers (1 Sam 17:26, 32, 35-37) and to Goliath himself (1 Sam 17:46-47). And David drew mockery from both the Israelites and Goliath (1 Sam 17:28, 33, 43-44). He was called conceited and weak by his own people, but he didn't care what he looked like to everyone else; he knew it was God's fight and his own weakness didn't matter. So David walked out toward Goliath with laughter both behind and before him and defeated the serpent.

As a result, David did end up winning the honor of the people of Israel, but only after first giving it up. This is how honor works for God's people; he who saves his life will lose it... and the humble will be exalted (Matt 10:39, 23:12). David literally crushed Goliath's skull, sinking a large stone into his forehead (1 Sam 17:49). David then took Goliath's own sword, cut his head off and carried it to Jerusalem.

Jerusalem at the time was controlled by the Jebusites. Normally, the head of a defeated enemy would be taken to the capital city to the cheers of the citizens. Saul ruled from Gibeah, which was north of Jerusalem, while David was from Bethlehem which was just south of Jerusalem. There are a couple possible reasons why David went to Jerusalem. It could very well have been a warning to the Jebusites who ruled there, as if to say, "You're next." Beyond this, David might have been staking a claim on the city he would later make his capital.

Fast forward to the crucifixion of Jesus at Golgotha. Golgotha is said to mean "the place of a skull" (Matt 27:33). The word Golgotha is related to the Hebrew word for skull: *gulguleth*, but there is an additional layer of meaning that helps everything make sense. Golgotha is also a contraction of Goliath of Gath. Golgotha is probably the place just outside of Jerusalem where David put the skull of Goliath on display. Jesus crushed the head of the serpent on the cross in the same place David put the head of this Philistine serpent.

APPLICATION

We tend to think that humility means sitting on the sidelines and not drawing attention to ourselves, and it often does work this way. But true humility is seeking the Lord's honor instead of our own. When David showed up on the battle lines to bring food to his brothers, he found that Goliath was shaming God's name, and the Israelites were trembling in fear... shamefully. To David, the nature of the situation was obvious: send a man out there who trusts the Lord and God will give him victory because His name is being shamed. Since no one else manned up, David volunteered. This drew attention to David, but that's not why he did it; in fact, he got mocked in the process. He was trusting that the Lord would defend His own name through him. As a result, God's honor was restored, and David was honored as well.

The lesson here is that God will defend His name *through* those who trust Him. This requires courage, but when God's name is being dishonored, step up in faith and be used by God.

ACTIVITIES

1. Make a Sling. The point of this activity is for you to get a sense of the power of David's sling. You will need the following:

Unit 8: The United Kingdom

- half a pant leg's worth of denim
- 6' of 3/8" rope
- super glue
- a pair of scissors
- a hole punch

1. Using the pattern on page 38, cut out two pieces of denim for your slingshot.

2. Super glue the two denim pieces together to make a seam, overlap them 1/2 to 1 inch. Glue them together in such a way to make a slightly cupped larger piece with the two pieces.

3. Using a hole punch, punch two holes in the seamed part about 1 inch from each end.

4. Cut the rope into two 3' pieces; run the rope strands through the holes on the ends and tie them back together about 4 inches up on the rope, a good double overhand knot will do the trick.

2. In David's Shoes. Read the following while imagining what it would have been like to be David. Then answer the questions that follow.

> You arrive at Israel's front line midday; the sky is overcast and the air is filled with the smell of smoldering campfires from the night before. Israel's shield-bearers are standing side-by-side, ready to move forward. Behind the shield-bearers, the archers and swordsmen stand in their companies in hushed fear. Some groups of men are talking quietly; some are standing in silence. The day has not gone as planned. You know that Israel's army is superior to the Philistine's in many ways; the Israelite men are well-trained and battle-hardened; their numbers are matched well with the Philistine's. By far the Israelites' greatest advantage is their righteous indignation—they hate the Philistines with a fierce hatred. The Philistines have ravaged their cities over the years, extorted tribute, killed their women and children and mocked Yahweh Who gave this land to His people.
>
> But what happened that morning had taken the Israelites by surprise. Instead of facing their enemies on the battlefield before them, one lone Philistine came out in front and stood between Israel's army and the Philistine's. He was huge, covered neck-down with impenetrable scale-armor, and he held a gigantic spear in his hand. He mocked Israel and called them to send forth a mighty warrior to face him. Instead of a battle of wits, guts, experience and anger on the battlefield, Goliath made this into a battle of honor between him and one lone Israelite. As soon as he issued this challenge, the whole Israelite army turned to King Saul, who was smaller than Goliath, but the closest thing they had to a giant. But instead of leading Israel with courage, Saul put his head in his hands and turned around in fear to return to his tent. The whole army followed his lead and began to quake in fear.

Lesson 8.4

As you walk up to the battle line, food in hand for your brothers, you struggle to figure out what's going on. You see a group of archers talking quietly and ask them what's going on. They just push you away. "What's a boy doing on the battlefield?" they ask. You move your way through the men and stand just behind the front line. As you peer between two men, you see the giant and hear his voice ring out again across the battlefield with the challenge he had issued over and over again that morning, "Who has the strength and courage to face me? If you can defeat me, you win the battle, if not, the battle goes to the Philistines!"

What did you feel as you imagined what David was going through? _____
_____
_____
_____
_____
_____

What do you think David was feeling? _____
_____
_____
_____
_____
_____

Why was David able to act so differently than every other Israelite? _____
_____
_____
_____
_____
_____
_____

Unit 8: The United Kingdom

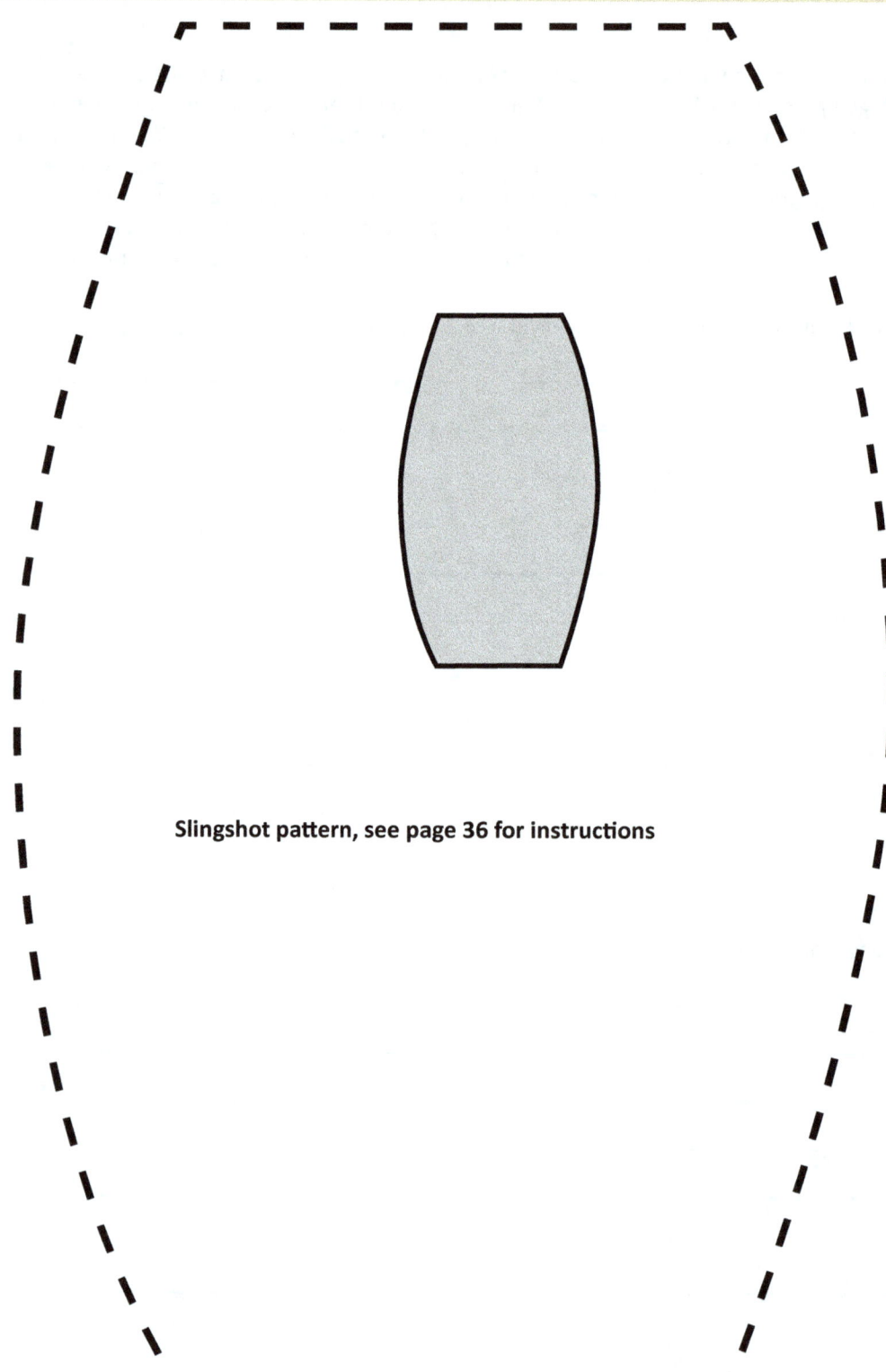

Slingshot pattern, see page 36 for instructions

Lesson 8.4

EVALUATION

1. Who is the serpent in this story? How do we know? _____
_____
_____

2. Who should have gone up against Goliath? _____
_____

3. What kind of fight was Goliath looking for? _____
_____

4. Did David give Goliath an honor fight? _____
_____
_____

5. What happened to David as a result of refusing Saul's armor and going after Goliath with a sling and some stones? _____
_____
_____
_____

6. How did people see David after the fight? _____
_____
_____

7. What did David do with Goliath's head? Why? _____
_____
_____

8. What does David bringing Goliath's head to Jerusalem have to do with Jesus dying on the cross?___
_____
_____
_____

LESSON 8.5

David's Tabernacle

UNIT 8

THE STORY

Lesson Theme - Israel began to be a light to the Gentiles.

This lesson is about how Israel began to fulfill their destiny as a light to the Gentiles, but that could only happen when individuals started to love God and walk with Him. This lesson is the story of two men who wanted to be in the presence of the God of Israel.

The first man, David, had been raised to walk with God and had followed God literally from childhood. God made him king over all Israel and gave him a capital city from which to govern—the first in Israel's history. David wanted to be in God's presence and to have God's presence at the very center of his kingdom; so he made a place for God's dwelling (the ark of the covenant) in the capital city with him.

The second man, Obed-Edom, was born in Gath, Goliath's hometown. He would have grown up worshiping idols. Somewhere along the line—perhaps when David was in Philistia, hiding from Saul—Obed-Edom encountered the God of Israel. He wanted to be closer to Yahweh, so he came to Israel and settled near Jerusalem. He probably thought he was as close as he would ever get to the capital city, but then Uzzah died and all of a sudden the ark of God was in his house. Obed-Edom and his family were tremendously blessed because of the ark (2 Sam 6:11), and when it went up to Jerusalem, he went too, finding a place as an adopted Levite, a doorkeeper in the new tabernacle.

OVERVIEW

David installed the ark of the covenant in a new tabernacle on Mt. Zion in his capital city, Jerusalem. He instituted a service of musical offerings that consciously mirrored the Levitical animal sacrifices and involved Gentiles in the worship, fulfilling in a new way Abraham's commission to be a blessing to the nations.

SOURCE MATERIAL

- 2 Samuel 6 (especially verses 17-19)
- 1 Chronicles 16
- Amos 9:1-15 (note verses 11 and 12)
- Acts 15:13-21 (note verse 16)
- Psalm 84
- Proverbs 14:34
- Leithart, *From Silence to Song*

Psalm 84 ties these two men together—coming from very different places and very different backgrounds, both of them just wanted to be as near to God as possible, and God made their dreams come true.

Drawing near to God in worship was always possible for Israel. The amazing thing was that it was also possible for Obed-Edom, the Gentile from Gath, to worship God. The building of David's tabernacle made that possible, and Amos prophesied that God would build it again (i.e., again include the Gentiles in worship just like the

Unit 8: The United Kingdom

OBJECTIVES

Feel...

- pleasure that Israel's mission to the Gentiles (that's most of us!) was finally being fulfilled in David's tabernacle.
- awe that David's tabernacle became a symbol that James could draw on 900 years later.
- the joy of Psalm 84 at the opportunity to be even just a doorkeeper in God's house rather than live among the wicked.

Understand...

- that the musical service in David's tabernacle paralleled the animal sacrifice service in the tabernacle at Shiloh.
- the "detective work" needed to determine that Gentiles were involved in the worship at David's tabernacle.
- the significance of Gentile involvement in tabernacle worship (fulfilling Abraham's commission to be a blessing).
- why James used the Amos prophecy as a validation that Gentiles could be part of God's people.
- that we can enter God's presence in a way that even the Jews couldn't do back in Old Testament days (and so the joy of Psalm 84 goes double for us now).

Apply this understanding by...

- thanking God for fulfilling His promises to Abraham so that all of us can join in being part of His people without having to be Jews first.
- thanking God that you have the privilege of entering God's presence in ways that even the Jews couldn't do back in the time of the Old Testament.

people of God) (Amos 9:1-15). Through the Holy Spirit, God made it possible for Gentiles to worship Him, first by causing the disciples to speak with Gentile languages at Pentecost (Acts 2) and then by sending the gospel out to the Gentiles (Acts 10-11). During the Jerusalem council, James pointed to this prophecy and through it to David's tabernacle, demonstrating that God's purpose had always been for Gentiles to worship Him (Acts 15:13-21).

David brought the ark up to Jerusalem, and he offered dedicatory sacrifices (2 Sam 6:17; 1 Chr 16:1); but after these initial sacrifices, there were no more animal sacrifices in David's tabernacle. David, however, instituted a service of song. He didn't simply make up something that seemed right to him; his service of musical offerings paralleled the structure of the animal sacrificial services that once took place at Shiloh, and were currently taking place in the tabernacle on the high place at Gibeon. 1 Chronicles 16 consciously plays up the parallels between the song service and the animal sacrificial service, going so far as to use the same Hebrew word for the musical *instruments* as Leviticus uses to describe the flesh-hooks, bowls and other *instruments* of animal sacrifice.

Another indication of the parallels that guided David is the "songs of ascents" in the book of Psalms (Pss 120-134). The word translated "ascents" is the Hebrew word 'olah. The same word is translated "burnt offering" or "whole burnt offering" in the Torah; but 'olah doesn't mean "whole"; it doesn't mean "burnt"; and it doesn't mean "offering." It means "to ascend," and describing an offering, the best translation is "ascension offering." In the Levitical tabernacle, this was a *great* description. (See Exod 29, Lev 1, and Lesson 5.9 for more information on the ascension offering.) Remember that the glory cloud hovered night and day over the tabernacle. When the Israelites made an offering, they didn't have to just take it on faith that God had received their offering: they could actually watch the offering burn and the smoke ascend to the glory cloud of God. The ascension offerings were made up of meat and oil, grain and wine, and they were offered every morning and every evening—consumed by fire on the altar and ascended to God in the smoke. David wrote "ascension songs" to parallel these offerings. These songs would be sung every morning and evening as musical offerings to the Lord, while on the high place in Gibeon, the priests would continue to offer animal sacrifices on the tabernacle altar (1 Chr 16:39-40).

In the next lesson, we will see how in Solomon's temple the musical service would be united to the animal sacrificial service. Until then, the musical service David designed stood on its own. But the really cool part is that *Gentiles were included*.

It takes a little detective work in order to grasp the main point of this lesson, that the Gentiles were included in tabernacle worship. When Uzzah died, David stashed the ark at the nearest convenient location, which happened to be the house of Obed-Edom the Gittite (2 Sam 6:10) (a Gittite is a person from Gath, and therefore, a Philistine). Although from David's perspective, Obed-Edom's was simply the closest house, placing the ark in a Gentile's house was providential and noteworthy. Yahweh had chosen to live with Gentiles since returning from Philistia: first with the Gibeonites of Kirjath Jearim and now with Obed-Edom the Philistine.

When David set up the musical worship that would take place in the new tabernacle, however, he demonstrated an understanding of Yahweh's invitation to Gentiles to join in worshiping Him. Listed among the doorkeepers of the tabernacle is...Obed-Edom (1 Chr 16:38). This was not a common name and an extremely unlikely name for an Israelite, since it means "servant of Edom." The most likely scenario is that Obed-Edom the Gittite, who had been blessed by the ark's presence in his home, was adopted into the Levite clan and became part of the tabernacle staff.

Psalm 84 is a meditation on the pleasure of being present in the sanctuary. It includes the line, "I would rather be a doorkeeper in the house of my God than dwell in the tents of wickedness" (Ps 84:10)—which is exactly the choice that Obed-Edom made. Furthermore, according to the superscription of the psalm, it was a song by the sons of Korah (who were in charge of keeping the doors of David's tabernacle; see 1 Chr 9:19), to be played on the *instrument of Gath* (Obed-Edom's home town).

Back when God made His original promises to Abraham, He promised that through Abraham, all the families of the earth would be blessed. In the Law of Moses, formal service in the tabernacle was a privilege reserved to the tribe of Levi, so a Gentile being adopted into the tabernacle staff is a *really* big deal, and there's more to come.

Amos prophesied that God would rebuild David's tabernacle that had fallen down (Amos 9:11). This meant that Yahweh would again receive worship that included the Gentiles. James, in turn, quoted Amos' prophecy at the close of the Acts 15 controversy in order to drive home the conclusion that Gentiles need not become Jews first in order to be good Christians and members of God's people. The apostles' conclusion in Acts 15 anticipates the scene in Revelation 5:9-10, where people from every tribe, language and nation worship God together. But it all started long ago in Jerusalem, at David's tabernacle.

Unit 8: The United Kingdom

APPLICATION

We can draw near to God today just like David and Obed-Edom did, no matter what our circumstances, no matter where we were born or what nationality or religion we were born into. Jesus died for all of us, and invites all of us to be His disciples. When we, from our various tribes and nations, draw near to God together, we begin to show the world a picture of the Amos prophecy: the whole world united in service to God.

ACTIVITIES

1. Sing Psalm 84. Psalm 84 is a meditation on the pleasure of being present in the sanctuary. It includes the line, "I would rather be a doorkeeper in the house of my God than dwell in the tents of wickedness,"—which is exactly the choice that Obed-Edom made. And according to the superscription, it is a song by the sons of Korah (who were in charge of keeping the doors of David's tabernacle; see 1 Chr 9:19), to be played on the instrument of Gath (Obed-Edom's hometown). Sing or read Psalm 84 and meditate on it. Write your reflections in the space below.

2. Draw It: David's Tabernacle. Draw a picture of David's tabernacle in the space below. Include a visualization of the songs of ascent rising up to God's presence like an offering (you don't have to be very detailed about all the tabernacle furnishings). Be creative in your drawing. As an added challenge, incorporate in your drawings that Gentile worshipers were also present at David's tabernacle.

Unit 8: The United Kingdom

EVALUATION

1. What was the ascension offering and why was it called that? _____
   _____
   _____
   _____

2. What is a song of ascent and why was it called that? _____
   _____
   _____
   _____

3. Who was Obed-Edom and where was he from? _____
   _____
   _____
   _____
   _____

4. How does Psalm 84 relate to Obed-Edom and David's tabernacle? _____
   _____
   _____
   _____
   _____

5. What did it mean when Amos prophesied that God would restore the fallen tabernacle of David? _____
   _____
   _____

6. Why did James quote the Amos prophecy? _____
   _____
   _____
   _____

LESSON 8.6

Solomon's Temple

UNIT 8

THE STORY

Lesson Theme - Israel continued to serve Yahweh under Solomon.

The major point of this lesson is that the nation of Israel continued to serve Yahweh under Solomon as it had under David, reaching a pinnacle of development. But this kind of national obedience doesn't just happen; it is always a result of particular choices by particular people. In this case, this is the story of a father who wanted to do something great for God, but wasn't able to do it. He passed the job on to his son, and his son faithfully completed the task that his father had given him.

David had achieved success. He was installed in Jerusalem, his new capital city. He lived in a palace there, and God had united Israel under his rule. God had consented to come and dwell in the same city, in a tabernacle built for the ark of the covenant. At this point, there was very little David could want that he didn't already have. He was on top of the world.

Then David realized that although he dwelt in luxury, he was allowing the God of the universe to live in a tent. That didn't seem right to him, and he wanted to change it (2 Sam 7:1-2). Shouldn't God have a better house than the king?

David shared his idea with Nathan the prophet, and Nathan said, "Go, do all that is in your heart, for the LORD is with you" (2 Sam 7:3). But that night, God told Nathan something a little different. You can read the whole speech in 2 Samuel 7:5-16, but in sum, the message was this: "David, you think *you* are going to build *My* house? No,

OVERVIEW

Since leading Israel up out of Egypt, Yahweh had always dwelt among them in a tent, never in a permanent building. David wanted to build a house for God, and God responded by promising to build David's house into an everlasting dynasty. However, Yahweh didn't let David do the work of building the temple himself. He allowed David to make plans and gather materials for the temple, but commanded that Solomon be the one to build it. In Solomon's temple, regular animal sacrifices were resumed and united to the musical service David had created, and Israel joined in worshiping God together.

SOURCE MATERIAL

- 2 Samuel 7
- 1 Kings 5-8
- 1 Chronicles 22, 28-29
- 2 Chronicles 2-7
- Psalm 132
- Proverbs 1:8, 28:7

I am going to build *your* house like you've never imagined!"

In addition, God conveyed to David that because he was a man of war, God didn't want him to build the temple, but He would let David's son build it (2 Chr 22:6-10). You can read David's own account of God's revelation to him in 1 Chronicles 22:5-10 and 28:2-8. So David gathered materials, made preparations, offered sacrifices

49

Unit 8: The United Kingdom

> **OBJECTIVES**
>
> **Feel...**
>
> - David's awe at God's graciousness toward him.
> - awe at God's acceptance and consecration of the temple.
>
> **Understand...**
>
> - why David felt awkward living in a palace while God lived in a tent.
> - how God rewarded David's good intentions by building David's house.
> - why God didn't let David build the temple, but had Solomon do it instead.
> - how the temple corresponds to the tabernacle and the garden of Eden.
>
> **Apply this understanding by...**
>
> - meditating on how God has been gracious to you.
> - considering how God gives people different blessings and calls people to different stations in life.
> - considering what your parents are asking of you at this point in your life and evaluating whether you are honoring your parents' instruction (if appropriate).

(1 Chr 29) and even received the plans from the Spirit (1 Chr 28:11-12), but he left the work of construction to his son.

The account of Solomon's work on the temple is found in 2 Chronicles 2-4 and 1 Kings 5-7. When the work was complete, Solomon brought the ark into the temple (2 Chr 5, 1 Kgs 8:1-21), gave a speech and dedicatory prayer (2 Chr 6, 1 Kgs 8:22-61), and made dedicatory sacrifices (2 Chr 7:1-11, 1 Kgs 8:62-66).

Notice that God signified His acceptance of the temple by kindling the fire on the altar Himself (2 Chr 7:1), which happened periodically throughout the Old Testament (Lev 9:24, 1 Chr 21:26, 1 Kgs 18:38), including at the dedication of the tabernacle (Lev 9). As God had accepted the tabernacle, so He also accepted the temple as His dwelling place.

The temple was constructed on the same basic template as the tabernacle, with an innermost Holy of Holies that contained the ark; the Holy Place containing the lampstands, showbread tables, and altar of incense; and a veil dividing the two chambers. Instead of one outer court, as in the tabernacle, the temple had two.

The temple was greater than the tabernacle in every measurable respect. It was bigger. It was richer. It was a permanent structure instead of a tent. The altar was huge. Instead of the man-portable bronze laver, it had the bronze sea, 15 feet in diameter, 7 ½ feet deep and made entirely of cast bronze. Instead of one lampstand and one table of showbread, there were ten of each. In other words, the temple was an upgrade, and a big one. In fact, there was so much invested in the sacrificial equipment of the temple that it wasn't even accounted for (1 Kgs 7:47) (can you imagine that, in a building project?).

The temple was decorated like the tabernacle was, with garden motifs inside and out, and cherubim overshadowing the ark. As the tabernacle was, the temple was a garden of Eden, but not a portable one like the tabernacle. At David's request, God had chosen a permanent place to dwell and commune with mankind on Mt. Moriah, as He had once dwelt in the mountain sanctuary of Eden and communed with man in the garden.

APPLICATION

Proverbs 1:8 and 28:7 reflect on how a son who hears his father's instruction and lives well will be a delight to his father. At this stage of his life, Solomon exemplified these things. If you are still living with your parents and under their guidance and authority, think through how well you are doing at honoring their direction. If you are past that stage of life, reflect on ways your parent's training has affected you over the years.

ACTIVITIES

1. Count Your Blessings. Reflect on what life is like in a third-world country and count your own blessings.

> Consider a coastal fisherman's family on a small island in Indonesia: Dad, Mom, and five kids. They all live in a small village in a one-room hut made of bamboo. When it's hot, they're hot; when it's cold, they're cold. They can warm up around the fire, but first they have to go out and cut firewood or pick up driftwood along the beach. If they catch fish that day, they eat; if not, they go hungry. They wear clothing made of pounded tree bark—maybe they can buy 'normal' clothes if they can catch enough fish to sell and make a little money—and if they can get the fish to market without getting robbed by bandits. When they have to go to the bathroom, they use a little outhouse 50 yards away from the house, so they don't have to smell the stink. Even then, on hot days, if the wind is blowing the wrong direction.... If they have to go in the middle of the night and it's raining, they have to either hold it 'til morning, or go out and walk 50 yards in the rain. They wipe with leaves collected along the way. At any time, pirates could come to take what little they have, kill the men, rape the women, and steal the children to sell. They keep weapons to defend themselves, but guns are expensive. Maybe one of the men in the village has an old rifle left over from WWII and a few bullets. Other than that, all they have are knives and sticks. In this family, Dad has an old sword. And there are only four or five families in the whole village; most pirate crews have at least as many men as are in the village and all of them skilled, well-armed fighters. (This is a real issue, by the way: piracy is a way of life for many of the warlike tribes of coastal Indonesia.)

Make a list below of all the ways God blesses you in a typical day. Include everything from friends, to sanitation to security, and anything else you can think of. _____

_____

_____

_____

Unit 8: The United Kingdom

_____

_____

_____

Having compiled that list of blessings in one single day, sit back and take it all in. This is God's blessing in a single day. How great is that? When David offered to build the temple for God to dwell in, God responded with a promise to build David's house. He promised David that He would take care of his family and keep his descendants on the throne, not just for one day, but forever. Spend some time in prayer, thanking God for how well He takes care of you.

2. Personal Reflection Answer the following questions.

Why wasn't David allowed to build the temple? _____

_____

_____

_____

Didn't God bring David into the whole situation with Goliath? David didn't go looking for trouble; God led him into that situation. Didn't David do the right thing? _____

_____

_____

_____

So if David was doing what God called him to do, then why wouldn't God let him build the temple? That's not fair, is it? _____

_____

_____

_____

How does this apply to our lives? _____

_____

_____

_____

Lesson 8.6

What are examples of good things God might call someone to do that keep that person from doing other good things? _____

_____

_____

_____

_____

_____

_____

3. Journal Time. Make a list in the space below of the things God requires of you in a typical day. Include things that your God-given authorities require of you as well as things that are just between you and God. Next to each item in the list, rate yourself on a scale of 1-10: how well are you doing at honoring God as you keep that obligation? _____

Unit 8: The United Kingdom

EVALUATION

1. Why did David feel awkward about God living in a tent in Jerusalem? _____
_____
_____

2. What did David want to do? _____
_____
_____

3. How did God respond? _____
_____
_____

4. Why was Solomon allowed to build the temple?_____
_____
_____

5. Compare and contrast the temple with the tabernacle of David and the original tabernacle that Moses built. _____
_____
_____
_____
_____
_____
_____

UNIT 9: THE DIVIDED KINGDOM

Solomon continued to worship Yahweh all his life, but he married many foreign wives and began to worship their false gods as well. Because he had fallen away from worshiping Yahweh alone, Yahweh took ten tribes of Israel away from Solomon's family and gave them to Solomon's servant, Jeroboam. Yahweh promised to make Jeroboam's family king over the ten tribes forever if Jeroboam would serve Him, but Jeroboam instituted false worship and caused Israel to sin. Meanwhile, instead of repenting, Solomon's son Rehoboam chose to make the same mistakes as his father.

The kings of the north followed the precedent set by Jeroboam, who had established the northern kingdom. The best of the northern kings, Jehu, was hand-picked by God to cleanse Baal worship out of Israel, and he did an outstanding job. But even Jehu perpetuated the false worship that eventually brought about Israel's downfall.

Meanwhile in the south, the kings of Judah had oscillated in their faithfulness to God ever since Solomon; many served idols, and a few served Yahweh. Of those few, most allowed the people to continue in idolatry, but there were a few reformers. The last and probably most effective of these was King Josiah. Under Josiah, Judah rediscovered the Law and renewed their oath to keep it. Josiah destroyed the idols and temples to false gods as far north as Samaria and insisted that the people worship Yahweh alone. However, when Josiah died, his son returned to worshiping idols, and eventually God allowed the southern kingdom to be taken captive into Babylon.

When He sent Judah into exile in Babylon, Yahweh promised that He would bring them back after 70 years, and He fulfilled His promise through a three-wave process. Zerubbabel brought back the first wave of people and rebuilt the temple. Ezra led the second wave of people, beautified the temple and brought reforms where the people had fallen into sin. Nehemiah led a third wave of restoration, rebuilding the wall and further reforming the spiritual life of the nation.

LESSON 9.1

Jeroboam's Revolt

UNIT 9

THE STORY

Lesson Theme - Israel declined because of Solomon's disobedience.

In this lesson, we learn the story of three kings: Solomon, his son Rehoboam, and Solomon's servant Jeroboam. Solomon departed from the Lord, and so the Lord promised to take most of the kingdom away from his family and give it to Jeroboam instead. When Solomon's son Rehoboam inherited the throne, he made the same mistakes his father had, and God fulfilled His promise, making Jeroboam king over the ten northern tribes of Israel. But Jeroboam did not serve God either, and Rehoboam continued in his father's errors instead of taking a lesson from God's judgment of his father and repenting.

Solomon started out well, but things went south when he began to marry foreign women (1 Kgs 11:1-6). Solomon was a man of peace, but rather than relying on the Lord to protect his kingdom, he made alliances. In those days, you didn't just make an alliance by signing a treaty—you also intermarried with the nation you were making the treaty with. So Solomon was making alliances with all the kings around him and marrying their daughters to seal the peace treaties. Everybody did it this way back then. In other words, Solomon was doing what everyone else did instead of trusting God.

The result is predictable: Solomon's heart was turned away to idols, and since he was the king and a great builder, he ended up building temples to idols in Jerusalem (1 Kgs 11:7-8). God quite properly hated Solomon's idolatry and

OVERVIEW

Solomon continued to worship Yahweh all his life, but he married many foreign wives and began to worship their false gods as well. Because he had fallen away from worshiping Yahweh alone, Yahweh took ten tribes of Israel away from Solomon's family and gave them to Solomon's servant, Jeroboam. Yahweh promised to make Jeroboam's family king over the ten tribes forever if Jeroboam would serve Him, but Jeroboam failed and caused Israel to sin. Meanwhile, instead of repenting, Solomon's son Rehoboam chose to make the same mistakes as his father.

SOURCE MATERIAL

- 1 Kings 11-14
- Psalm 135
- Proverbs 1:8, 10:1, 17:25

judged Solomon for it. God raised up enemies for Solomon to deal with, including Jeroboam.

Jeroboam ultimately became God's major judgment upon Solomon. Because God had promised to David to extend his dynasty forever, God couldn't just take the kingdom away from Solomon as He had once taken it from Saul to give to David. But God could leave David's family two tribes and give away the other ten—and that's exactly what He promised Solomon He would do (1 Kgs 11:11-13). Just as King Saul had once tried to kill David, Solomon tried to kill Jeroboam—

Unit 9: The Divided Kingdom

OBJECTIVES

Feel...

- surprise that after such a good beginning, Solomon would fall away from God.
- surprise that after seeing God's judgment on Solomon's family, Jeroboam would fail the same test.
- a sense of betrayal that Jeroboam would abandon God after God had given him so much.

Understand...

- how Solomon failed and why God was judging him.
- why God didn't take the kingdom away from Solomon entirely.
- that Rehoboam lost the ten northern tribes because of his pride, taking the easy counsel instead of the wise counsel.
- why Jeroboam was afraid for his people to go to Jerusalem three times a year as the Lord had commanded.
- how God cursed Jeroboam as a result of his betrayal.

Apply this understanding by...

- considering what good lessons your parents have to teach that you need to learn.
- evaluating your sources of counsel and determining whether you take advice just because it's easy to follow or if you choose to take wise advice.
- considering whether you are willing to repent or are hard-hearted like Jeroboam was, refusing to repent despite the opportunities God gives you.

and like Saul, he failed, because God was with Jeroboam (1 Kgs 11:40).

In due course, Solomon died (1 Kgs 11:43), and the people heaved a sigh of relief. Building all those temples to idols was expensive business, and Solomon was raising all the money for it through taxes. Rehoboam came to the throne, and the people wanted his reign to be different than Solomon's. So they sent Rehoboam a delegation (which included Jeroboam), asking him not to behave like his father. Rehoboam asked for three days to think about it (1 Kgs 12:3-5).

Rehoboam's older counselors all told him to listen to the people. If he would serve them now, they would love him forever (1 Kgs 12:7). The younger counselors, however, told him to say, "My little finger will be thicker than my father's waist! And now, whereas my father put a heavy yoke on you, I will add to your yoke; my father chastised you with whips, but I will chastise you with scourges!" (1 Kgs 12:10-11). Their counsel appealed to him, and he went back and told the people that he would be even worse than his father. Rehoboam was taking the easy way here; if he had listened to his older counselors, he would have had to humble himself and serve the people—put their needs ahead of his own desires. By listening to his young counselors instead, he took the path of pride—and God resists the proud.

And so the people rebelled. The ten northern tribes refused to recognize Rehoboam as king. The nation was ready to have a civil war, but God commanded them to back off and accept the division, because He had authored it (1 Kgs 12:22-24). Indeed, God had already promised the ten northern tribes to Jeroboam. An uneasy peace descended, with Rehoboam ruling in the south and Jeroboam in the north.

Lesson 9.1

This division of the nation of Israel was God's promised judgment on Solomon, Rehoboam's father, for following foreign gods, and Rehoboam should have taken it as a wake-up call. If he had, then he could have destroyed the idols' temples, put away foreign gods, and God would have blessed him. Instead, Rehoboam was too hard-hearted, and he continued the sins of his father, worshiping foreign gods alongside Yahweh (1 Kgs 14:21-24).

Meanwhile, Jeroboam was facing a real political problem. Every male in Israel was required to go up to Jerusalem and appear before Yahweh three times a year at the pilgrim feasts (1 Kgs 12:25-27). But how was Jeroboam supposed to hold his kingdom together if his people were going three times a year into "enemy" territory to worship at the "enemy's" capital city? (Remember that nobody even considered separation of church and state back then—there was a national government and a national religion. And both church and state had the same capital, in Jerusalem.)

What Jeroboam should have done, of course, was trust God. God had promised him the kingdom, and it was God's job to keep His promise. All Jeroboam had to do was follow God. Instead of walking by faith, Jeroboam went for a solution he could see. He built two golden calves and set them up in Dan and Bethel, saying, "Here are your gods, O Israel, which brought you up from the land of Egypt!" (1 Kgs 12:28). He told the people that journeying all the way down to Jerusalem was much too far; they could just go to the golden calves instead. He set up a false priesthood to administer this false worship and caused the ten northern tribes to follow him in his rebellion against God (1 Kgs 12:28-33).

Jeroboam's actions set a terrible precedent. The northern kingdom would last for about 250 more years and would have 20 kings over that time-span. Some of them would be worse than others, but *every one of them* would repeat Jeroboam's sin, provoking God's judgment. (See 1 Kgs 16:26; 22:52; 2 Kgs 3:3; 10:29; 13:2; 13:11; 14:24; 15:9, 18, 24, 28; 17:21-23.)

In Jeroboam's lifetime, God responded to Jeroboam's idolatry in two ways. First, He sent an unnamed prophet up to the altar of the golden calf at Bethel (1 Kgs 13:1-5, 33-34). The prophet loudly cursed the altar and predicted that God would send Josiah to desecrate it (which came to pass—see 2 Kgs 23). Then the prophet said that as a sign of the altar's future desecration, God would split the altar now. King Jeroboam was before the altar himself when the prophet spoke these things. He pointed at the prophet and shouted, "Arrest him!" Immediately, the king's hand withered, and the altar split. In order to be healed, King Jeroboam had to humble himself, come to the prophet, and ask him to pray for healing. The prophet did so, and Jeroboam's hand was returned to normal—but Jeroboam did not repent.

God's second response came when Jeroboam's son became sick (1 Kgs 14:1-3). Jeroboam sent his wife down to the prophet Ahijah of Shiloh to seek healing for the boy. Ahijah was the same prophet who had delivered God's promise to make Jeroboam king, so Jeroboam trusted Ahijah. However, Jeroboam had also treated God very badly, so he told his wife to visit Ahijah in disguise. God revealed her identity to Ahijah and told him what to say to her. Ahijah delivered one of the harshest curses in the entire Bible; you can read it in 1 Kings 14:6-16.

Unit 9: The Divided Kingdom

APPLICATION

Take some time to reflect on how Israel became divided. Solomon violated one of the basic commands God had given to kings: not to multiply wives for themselves (Deut 17:14-17), and in the process he married a bunch of unbelievers. Solomon's disobedience caused a lot of damage that he didn't live to see. We don't have to contend with the temptation to marry 600 people today, but we certainly can make the same mistake by marrying one unbeliever.

It's important to seek advice, and Rehoboam did that. But what do you do when your advisors contradict each other, like Rehoboam's did? How do you know which advice to follow? There are few hard-and-fast rules, but here are some principles we can draw from Rehoboam's mistake. Generally, the counsel of older people is worth more. Counsel that requires humility and submission from you is more often right than counsel that lets you do whatever you want.

Meanwhile, we also need to learn a lesson in trusting God from Jeroboam's bad example. God *gave* him the ten northern tribes. Instead of trusting God to maintain the gift, Jeroboam made the golden calves in order to prevent the "threat" of his people having to go up to Jerusalem. When God calls you into a job, He will provide what you need along the way. It is possible to mess things up by failing to trust Him.

ACTIVITIES

1. Personal Reflection. Answer the following questions.

Who do you go to first when you need advice? Who do you go to next? _____

_____

Who gives you advice that's easy to follow? _____

_____

Who gives you advice that's hard to follow? _____

_____

How does it work out for you, depending on which advice you take? _____

_____

2. Journal Time: The Withered Hand. Think about the moment at the altar when Jeroboam had to ask the prophet to restore his withered hand. There was a moment, right there, when he had a chance to repent of everything and return to the Lord. He could have fixed everything, right there.

Lesson 9.1

How stupid was it that Jeroboam didn't fix everything when he could have? But then, why didn't he?
_____
_____

Are we so different? Think about a specific time when you've done the wrong thing and it turned out badly. Were there chances to repent along the way, before all the consequences caught up with you?
_____
_____

Why didn't you repent? _____
_____

EVALUATION

1. How did Solomon fail? Why did he fail in this way? _____
_____

2. What judgment did God promise to Solomon's family? _____
_____

3. Why didn't God just take away *all* the tribes from Solomon's family? _____
_____

4. How did Rehoboam lose the ten northern tribes? _____
_____

5. After God took the northern tribes away, did Rehoboam learn his lesson and repent? _____

6. How did Jeroboam do at serving God? _____
_____
_____

7. How did God respond to being betrayed by Jeroboam? _____
_____

LESSON 9.2

Jehu Cleansed Israel, Yet Still Failed

UNIT 9

THE STORY

Lesson Theme - Following the Lord fully

Historically, this lesson is the story of the *best* king the northern kingdom had and how even he failed to follow God all the way, which sets us up for understanding God's judgment on Israel. At its moral core, this lesson is about how it's possible to do great things for God without really following Him with your whole heart. Jehu took incredible risks and went to extraordinary lengths to rid Israel of Baal worship, but in the end he didn't actually take the leap of faith to fully follow the Lord.

The fact that Jehu stopped short is also a testament to the power of Jeroboam's precedent and furnishes another lesson: we never know how we'll influence people downstream of us. Jeroboam began a tradition of mixed worship that continued through a number of generations. Eventually, King Ahab came to the throne, and Ahab made the mistake that Solomon had made before him—he married a foreign wife, Jezebel of Sidon. The Sidonians were Baal worshipers, and Jezebel brought their worship in with a vengeance, leading almost the whole nation of Israel astray. The important point is that while all idol-worship is sin, some forms of idolatry have worse consequences than others. The northern kingdom started out idolatrous from the beginning, but over time it had gotten much worse.

God told Jehu to kill a lot of people, and in order to understand why, we need to remember Israel's covenant with God. Idolatry violated two of the Ten Commandments (Deut 5:7-8), and in

OVERVIEW

The kings of the north followed the precedent set by Jeroboam, who had established the northern kingdom. Jehu was one of the best of the northern kings: he was hand-picked by God to cleanse Baal worship out of Israel, and he did an outstanding job. But even he perpetuated the false worship that eventually brought about Israel's downfall.

SOURCE MATERIAL

- 2 Kings 9-10
- Psalms 4, 104, 115
- Ecclesiastes 5:18-20
- 1 Timothy 6:17

Israel, it was a capital crime (Deut 13:6-16, 17:2-5). Idolatry brought God's curse down on Israel (Deut 11:16-17), and God promised that if they insisted on worshiping idols, He would dispossess them just as He had the Canaanites (Deut 8:19-20).

Any idol worship is an abomination to God (Deut 12:29-31), but Baal worship was particularly nasty stuff. It involved human sacrifice of babies, bisexual orgies, religious prostitution, and more. God hated it and wanted it driven out of the land, but it was pervasive. Note God's comment to Elijah in 1 Kings 19:18 that He had 7,000 people who had not bowed the knee to Baal. In the context of Elijah thinking he was the only one left, 7,000 was a lot. In the context of a

Unit 9: The Divided Kingdom

OBJECTIVES

Feel...

- admiration for Jehu's zeal to cleanse Israel from Baal worship.
- disappointment that even Jehu failed to follow the Lord fully.

Understand...

- how Israel had gone far beyond Jeroboam's sins by getting involved in Baal worship.
- how much God hated Baal worship and wanted it cleaned out of Israel.
- that Jehu systematically exterminated Ahab's family first, without letting on that his goals were anything more than political.
- how Jehu then deceived the Baal worshipers and killed them all.
- that God rewarded Jehu for being obedient even though he did not fully follow God.
- how Jehu helped Israel repent of a really bad sin (Baal worship), but failed to get to the heart of the matter because he didn't lead the people to repent of *all* their idolatry.
- how Jehu's failure would ultimately doom the northern kingdom to destruction.

Apply this understanding by...

- recognizing the "gods" that people worship and then considering your own idolatrous tendencies.
- formulating a concrete plan for cultivating trust and gratitude in your own life in order to avoid idolatry.

whole nation, though, it was a tiny minority. By the time we get to Elijah, most of the nation had worshiped Baal at one time or another. It was so thoroughly entrenched that even Elijah's slaughter of 450 priests of Baal on Mt. Carmel hadn't stopped it. God's plan for cleansing Israel of Baal worshipers can be found in 1 Kings 19:15-18: God would use Hazael of Syria, Jehu, and Elisha to do the work.

This lesson is the story of Jehu, an army commander for King Joram, the son of Ahab and Jezebel. Ahab had died at this point, but Jezebel was still alive, and Joram, their son, was ruling. The story begins with Elisha and the "sons of the prophets" (2 Kgs 9:1), who were young men learning from Elisha how to serve as prophets. God had already told Elijah that He was going to make Jehu king, and Elijah had undoubtedly told Elisha. Now it was time to act on that information. Elisha called one of the sons of the prophets and sent him out to anoint Jehu. But Elisha told him to do it secretly and then to immediately flee.

The young man found Jehu sitting with the other captains of the army and took him aside to deliver his message (2 Kgs 9:6-10). Notice that the message was not just that Jehu would one day be king: it was a commission to destroy the house of Ahab. When Jehu returned to the captains, they asked what was so important, and Jehu tried to dodge the question, "You know the man and his babble" (2 Kgs 9:11b). (Note that Jehu's reply indicates that the young man was known to them—he had probably preached and/or prophesied publicly, enough to get a reputation.)

Somehow, the captains knew Jehu was lying and called him on it. Jehu then told them the truth. Upon hearing the prophecy, the other men took off their outer garments and put them under him on the steps (2 Kgs 9:12-13).

The clothing of the culture was a tunic and then an outer layer. When going to do any kind of work, a man would take off his outer garment, so that he would have freedom of movement. There's nothing immodest about wearing the tunic on its own, but in normal social situations, a man would wear the outer garment as well. Its fabric and decoration would indicate his position in society, the same way that today you can tell how much money someone has and what sort of people they hang out with by their clothes. For men like these—commanders of the army—the garments would be richly decorated (just like Joseph's coat of many colors); the garments were a display of the glory of their position. Putting their garments on the steps and then having Jehu sit on them was a symbol of submission to his rule. The men were literally building him a throne out of their glory; they were saying that they would support him and make him king.

Jehu was at Ramoth Gilead, and King Joram was in Jezreel. Jehu had his men seal up Ramoth Gilead so no one could get out to send word to the king that Jehu was conspiring against him, and then he immediately gathered some men and rode for Jezreel (2 Kgs 9:14-15).

We don't know how many men Jehu took with him, but apparently it was a sizable number, because it was enough that when the city watch saw them coming and told King Joram, he had them send a messenger to ask if they came in peace. What follows is a funny scene. Jehu told the messenger, "What have you to do with peace? Turn around and follow me" (2 Kgs 9:18), and the messenger joined Jehu's forces. When the messenger didn't come back, King Joram sent a second one, and the same thing happened. By this time, Jehu's forces were close enough that the city watch was able to recognize him from the way he drove his chariot.

King Joram himself had his chariot prepared, and he and his brother, Ahaziah, went out to meet Jehu. When King Joram met up with Jehu, he asked if he had come in peace, and Jehu said, "What peace, as long as the harlotries of your mother Jezebel and her witchcraft are so many?" (2 Kgs 9:22). When Joram turned to flee, Jehu killed him and had his body thrown into the field Ahab had stolen from Naboth.

Jehu then continued to Jezreel, where word had reached Jezebel. She put on her makeup, dressed up, and called down to him from a high window, "Is it peace...murderer of your master?" (2 Kgs 9:31). Jehu told her servants to throw her out of the window. Later, when he sent his servants to collect the body, they couldn't find anything but a skull, the feet, and the palms of her hands, because the dogs had already eaten her.

As Jehu went on to exterminate Ahab's entire family, he gave public credit to God for fulfilling the prophecy He had made through Elijah (2 Kgs 10:9-10). All this time, Jehu's actions appeared to be a simple military coup. It was common practice in that culture for a new king to kill anyone who might contest his right to the throne, which meant killing the former king's whole family and anyone else who was particularly loyal to him. So outside of Jehu's close confidants, nobody knew that Jehu was destroying Baal worship.

Once Ahab's family was gone, Jehu spread the word that he would serve Baal even more than Ahab had. He proclaimed a feast to Baal and commanded that all Baal worshipers throughout the whole land come to it. In fact, he told

Unit 9: The Divided Kingdom

them that he would kill any Baal worshiper who did not come. When they were gathered in the temple, Jehu commanded them to examine the ranks of worshipers and be sure that not even one Yahweh worshiper had crept in—this feast was only for Baal worshipers. When Jehu was sure that there were no Yawheh worshipers present, he had 80 picked troops slaughter all the Baal worshipers and destroy the temple, turning it into a garbage dump (2 Kgs 10:18-28).

Jehu's campaign against Baal worship was a resounding success: at God's command, he removed Baal worship from Israel entirely. Through the whole effort, God steadily strengthened him and gave him favor with his army and his people. God even rewarded him at the end by promising that he would have a dynasty to the fourth generation (2 Kgs 10:30).

This moment, right after the conclusion of the campaign against Baal and his worshipers, would have been the *perfect* moment for Jehu to destroy the golden calves and abolish the worship on the high places, thus undoing the damage Jeroboam had done. That was the next obvious step, and Jehu blew it. Instead of restoring the worship that God commanded, Jehu continued to perpetuate the sins of Jeroboam, allowing Israel to worship the golden calves (2 Kgs 10:29-31). This was a violation of the covenant (Deut 12:1-4), and it would have drastic consequences for Jehu's dynasty and for all of Israel down the road.

God kept His promise to give Jehu a dynasty to the fourth generation, but then He permanently destroyed the entire northern kingdom through the Assyrians. When God destroyed the northern kingdom, He did it because they worshiped idols and abandoned worshiping Him in the way they should (2 Kgs 17:5-23).

APPLICATION

The big application from this lesson is that *all* idolatry is dangerous, not just the really gross stuff. For us, this means that idolatry is not just about houses, cars, good looks, athletic talent, and the obvious things that we turn into idols. According to Paul (Col 3:5), covetousness is idolatry. So *anything* we covet is an idol.

Beyond that, James 1:16-17 tells us that every good thing is a gift from God. When we think of a good thing as "just there" rather than as God's gift, we are making it into an idol. For example, if a bowl of cookie dough ice cream makes you feel better after a hard day, this is a good gift from God. But there are two ways to approach that bowl of ice cream. If you say, "Thank you God for giving me this ice cream for me to enjoy," then you are thinking of it as God's good gift. If you say, "I just want to get home and have some ice cream so I can feel better," then you are depending on the ice cream to make you feel better, and the ice cream has become an idol. Anything you think of as having the power to help you or make you feel better *in itself,* rather than thinking of it as God's good gift to you, has become an idol. Anything you think you *have* to have without regard to God has become an idol. Anytime you don't get what you want, and instead of thinking, "I wonder how God is going to take care of me in this situation," you think, "Oh no! This is a disaster!"—there's an idol problem.

Obviously, you can't get rid of everything that might be an idol in your life. If your house has become an idol, that doesn't mean that God is calling you to be homeless. If food is an idol, that doesn't mean that God has called you to starve to death. But God certainly has called you to begin thanking Him for His good gifts and to maintain that thankful attitude throughout your life, day in and day out. Meditate on Ecclesiastes 5:18-20 with this in mind.

ACTIVITIES

1. Make a List: What We Worship. Think of some things that people worship and make a list below. Then answer the following questions.

Read James 1:16-17. What does it mean to take God's good gift for granted rather than receiving it as a gift from God? _____

_____

_____

Jehu's big sin was that he didn't remove all the idol worship. He got rid of the idol worship with the worst consequences, but he kept the other idols, and in the end, God destroyed his kingdom over it. How can we avoid making the same mistake Jehu made? _____

_____

_____

How can we enjoy God's good gifts—nice clothes, ice cream, cars, money, sports, whatever—without worshiping them? _____

_____

_____

2. Journal Time: Idols. Answer the questions below.

All idols are wrong, but are they all the same? _____

_____

_____

_____

_____

_____

Unit 9: The Divided Kingdom

So can we get away with some of the little idols?

Spend some time writing in the space below, confessing your idols (big and small) to God and asking Him to cleanse your heart of these idols. Be specific about the areas of idolatry in your life.

Spend some time thanking God for the good things He has given you that you might be tempted to worship rather than thank Him for. Write a prayer of gratitude in the space below.

Lesson 9.2

EVALUATION

1. How did Jehu get the idea to become king? _____
_____
_____

2. What did Jehu do to become king? _____
_____

3. Why did God call Jehu to become king? _____
_____

4. Did people know that God had called Jehu to become king in order to destroy Baal worship? _____
_____
_____

5. Why didn't Jehu tell them the truth? _____
_____
_____

6. How did Jehu destroy Baal worship? _____
_____
_____

7. How did God respond to Jehu destroying Baal worship in Israel? _____
_____
_____

8. Where did Jehu go wrong? _____
_____
_____

9. What did God do because of Jehu's failure? _____
_____
_____
_____

LESSON 9.3

Josiah Recovered True Worship in the South

UNIT 9

THE STORY

Lesson Theme - Josiah led Israel in a revival, but it didn't stick.

At the national level, this lesson is about how the southern kingdom was so far gone that even with the best of reformers placed as highly as possible, they didn't come to a lasting repentance. As the story of Josiah's life, this lesson is about how Josiah served God as well as he knew, and when God showed him more, he responded immediately and zealously.

Since Jeroboam's revolt, the united kingdom of the twelve tribes of Israel had been split in two. The northern kingdom kept the name Israel, and was made up of the ten tribes that God had given to Jeroboam to rule. The southern kingdom was made up of the tribes of Judah and Benjamin, and was known as the kingdom of Judah. Both kingdoms had descended rapidly into serious idolatry.

Josiah, the great-grandson of Hezekiah, came to the throne at age eight (2 Kgs 22:1). Hezekiah had been an effective reformer and had led the nation in serving Yahweh, but his son Manasseh was the worst idolater who ever sat on the throne, and Manasseh's son Amon was nearly as bad (2 Kgs 18-21). Josiah was an immediate improvement; he served Yahweh (2 Kgs 22:2).

Having no idea that God required worship of Him alone, Josiah did not banish idolatry from his kingdom. The fact that Josiah did not know that idolatry was wrong seems like an odd idea to us, because we've been reared in a society

OVERVIEW

Since Solomon, the kings of Judah had oscillated in their faithfulness to God; many served other gods, and a few served Yahweh. Of those few, most allowed the people to continue to serve other gods, but there were a few reformers. The last and probably most effective of these was King Josiah. Under Josiah, Judah rediscovered the Law and took an oath to keep it. Josiah destroyed the idols and temples to false gods as far north as Samaria and insisted that the people worship Yahweh alone. However, when Josiah died, his son returned to worshiping other gods, and eventually God allowed the southern kingdom to be taken captive into Babylon.

SOURCE MATERIAL

- 2 Kings 22-25
- 1 Corinthians 10:19-22
- Psalm 115
- Ecclesiastes 2:18-19

that has been Christian(ish) for 1,500 years. But in the ancient world, a person would worship many gods, each one with a different "specialty." If he got sick, he would make sacrifices to the appropriate god in order to get better. If his wife became pregnant, he would sacrifice to a different goddess to ensure a safe pregnancy. When he started important work, he would sacrifice to the gods of his trade. At city festivals, he would sacrifice to the gods of the city. At meals,

Unit 9: The Divided Kingdom

OBJECTIVES

Feel...

- surprise that the spiritual state of the nation had gotten so bad that even the priests had lost the Bible.
- sympathy that Josiah honestly didn't know he was breaking God's Law.

Understand...

- that the nation had spiritually declined to the point that Judah had *lost the Bible*.
- that Josiah was still following Yahweh wholeheartedly, as best as he knew how.
- that Josiah honestly didn't know that Yahweh wanted His people to worship Him *alone*.
- that Josiah responded to God as soon as he knew what to do and obeyed God thoroughly by putting away the idols.
- that God honored Josiah's obedience, but still judged the nation.
- that Yahweh is a jealous God and does not share worship with idols.

Apply this understanding by...

- continuing to consider your own potential idols.
- fasting from one potential idol for a day.

he might make a small sacrifice to the gods of the hearth and home. He might also sacrifice to patron gods who watched over his family. So one person might be making sacrifices to 50 different gods, depending on what he needed.

None of these gods required exclusive devotion. The pregnancy goddess didn't get mad if you sacrificed to the gods of the city; the gods of the city didn't get angry if you sacrificed to your family gods, and so on. Yahweh's demand for exclusive devotion was very unusual in the ancient world. So if Josiah didn't have the Bible to tell him, he would never have guessed that Yahweh hated idolatry.

Viewed from a solid biblical perspective, of course, Yahweh's position makes sense. An idol is a demon (1 Cor 10:19-22), and of course we cannot be worshiping the Lord of the universe while worshiping demons. The demons don't object to a person worshiping other demons—after all, they are all on the same side.

So Josiah worshiped Yahweh with his whole heart, but he had no sense that it wouldn't be okay for other people in the kingdom to be worshiping all kinds of other gods. But then, they found the Bible again...

When Josiah sent money for the upkeep and repair of the temple, the high priest told the scribe in charge of the money that he had found the book of the covenant between Israel and Yahweh. This may have been the whole Torah, but the specific reference is more likely to the book of Deuteronomy. The scribe read the book and then read it to Josiah (2 Kgs 22:8-10).

In order to understand Josiah's reaction, we have to understand just how bad things had gotten in Judah. Yahweh had banned all worship of other gods, but they had temples to other gods all over the place. Yahweh had given command after specific command not to worship the Canaanite deities, and they were worshiping them all. They even had a wooden idol set up in the temple of Yahweh itself! Yahweh had made the command against adultery one of the Ten Commandments, and they had prostitutes plying their trade *in the temple* (see 2 Kgs 23:4-8).

Deuteronomy specifically promised that if the nation did these things, God would throw them out of the land and drive them among the Gentile nations. See Deuteronomy 28:15-68 for the very vivid terms of the curse God had put on them, should they disobey.

Josiah heard all these things, immediately realized that the nation had been disobedient beyond imagination for generations, and he tore his clothes (a sign of deep grief in that society) (2 Kgs 22:11). He knew that they were in trouble, but he didn't know how much. So he sent a delegation to Huldah the prophetess of Yahweh, to have her speak to Yahweh for them.

Huldah responded that Yahweh would judge the land and its people as He had written in the book of the covenant, and He would not be swayed. Their unfaithfulness had gone too far and too long not to judge. But because Josiah's heart was tender and humble before God, He would allow Josiah to live out his days before the judgment would fall (2 Kgs 22:15-20).

Josiah immediately followed through on his new insight. He gathered all the people for a reading of the covenant and took the oath of the covenant himself, with the whole nation as witnesses (2 Kgs 23:1-3). The people joined him in the oath, and then he cleansed the temple of all the pagan instruments, idols, and prostitutes that were in it. He burned all the idols and moved on to the high places where various idols were worshiped around Jerusalem. He also destroyed all the pagan temples, including the ones that Solomon had built (2 Kgs 23:4-14).

Josiah also went as far north as Samaria to continue cleansing the land. There, he encountered the altar Jeroboam had built at Bethel (2 Kgs 23:15), and he burned the bones of the priests on it (desecrating the altar) and then destroyed it, fulfilling the prophecy that the unnamed prophet had made shortly after Jeroboam first inaugurated worship there (see 1 Kgs 13 and Lesson 9.1 for details). Josiah did the same for all the altars and high places in the north.

Returning to Jerusalem, Josiah commanded that Judah keep the Passover as the covenant required of them (2 Kgs 23:21). Then the nation observed a Passover such as they had not had since the days of the Judges. (The comment in 2 Kgs 23:22 is about the quality of the feast; it isn't saying that Israel had never observed the Passover since the Judges. We know, for example, that Hezekiah kept the Passover—see 2 Chr 30). This all happened in the 18th year of Josiah's reign: the discovery of the Law, the cleansing of the temple and the land, the Passover, all of it. Josiah's obedience was not just thorough, it was also very prompt.

Josiah continued to follow the Law throughout the rest of his life and died at the age of 39. He reigned in Judah for 31 years, keeping the whole Law for the last 13 years of his reign.

However, Josiah's reforms didn't hold. His son Jehoahaz reigned after him and returned to idol worship (2 Kgs 23:32). Pharaoh Necho came up and imprisoned Jehoahaz after only three months and made his brother Jehoiakim king in his place, but he was just as bad (2 Kgs 23:37). Jehoiakim was forced to serve first Pharaoh Necho and then Nebuchadnezzar of Babylon. Throughout Jehoiakim's reign, he was beset by raiders from Syria, Chaldea, and Moab, because God had determined to destroy Judah as He had

Unit 9: The Divided Kingdom

promised (2 Kgs 24:1-2). When Jehoiakim died, his son Jehoiachin reigned in his place for three months before Babylon besieged Jerusalem. Jehoiachin eventually surrendered to Nebuchadnezzar, who looted the city and the temple and carried the plunder back to Babylon. He also took Jehoiachin, the royal family, the warriors and craftsmen captive from Jerusalem (2 Kgs 24:12-16).

Nebuchadnezzar left Zedekiah in charge in Jehoiachin's place, but he was evil as well (2 Kgs 24:19); after 11 years Zedekiah rebelled against Babylon. The Babylonian army came, destroyed Jerusalem, and carried the entire southern kingdom into captivity (2 Kgs 25:1-21).

APPLICATION

Obviously, we can learn a lot from Josiah. He sought the Lord, and the Lord rewarded him with further understanding (finding the book of the covenant). Josiah responded immediately, fully, and zealously to God's covenant, and God rewarded him again. The lesson from Josiah's quick obedience is valuable, and it's where you ought to spend your time on application.

We also need to notice that time does not dissolve covenantal obligations or make sin better. Josiah could have said, "Wow, that book is really interesting reading, but Deuteronomy was a really long time ago. Things have kinda changed—everybody worships a lot of different gods now." Or he could have said, "Wow, this is really bad, but we've been doing it for so long, what's the point of trying to change now?" Often, if a sin has been going on for long enough in our lives, we either feel like it must be okay, or we feel like it's hopeless to try to address it *now*. Instead of falling into those temptations, Josiah immediately recognized that Israel had been failing at their obligations for generations, and repented immediately. So should we.

In terms of God's character, this lesson brings home a theme repeated often in the Torah: Yahweh is a jealous God. In our society, we tend to think of jealousy as entirely a bad thing, but it isn't. Jealousy in the good sense means forcefully defending the relationship that legitimately belongs to you. If a man cheats on his wife, she should be jealous; if she's not, something is deeply wrong with their relationship. Likewise, Judah cheated on Yahweh. She owed Him *all* her worship, and when she gave some of her worship to idols, He was jealous—and rightly so. The same thing happens when we begin to worship our cell phones, our computers, our clothes, our athletic or academic ability, our popularity....

Psalm 115 is a meditation on idolatry and makes the point in vivid terms that we become like what we worship. As human beings, God has made us to realize our full potential as the image of God, and we do that by worshiping Him. If we worship something else, we become something less than what we could and should be. The psalm employs the perennial biblical strategy of mocking the idol. One useful way to mock an idol is to compare and contrast it with Jesus (see Activity 2).

The other part of application is found in Ecclesiastes 2:18-19: you can't predict your legacy. Josiah worked hard to bring the nation of Judah back to the Lord, but after he died, Judah went in a different direction. The same thing will happen with in your life: you never know what others with do with your legacy when you are gone.

ACTIVITIES

1. Idolatry Fast. In the last few lessons we've been focusing on idolatry, and how people can worship all kinds of things, not just little statues of supposed gods. In one way, Josiah had it easy. The idols he was dealing with were all things that he could just destroy. The things we worship—money, cell phones, computers, cars, clothes and so on—are things we need to function in everyday life. We can't just throw them all away...or can we? Throughout Christian history, there have been a few people who did their best to give up all those comforts that people worship, but that's always been an extreme choice that most people just can't really do. However, Christians have often chosen a less extreme way of reminding ourselves that we can live without these things: fasting. Choose one thing that you are tempted to worship, and go without it for a day. Be flexible and creative. The following tips and guidelines will help you understand how to go about fasting from an idol.

- If your well-fitting and fashionable clothes are the idol, of course you can't go without, but you can fast from your fashionable wardrobe for a day. Try wearing clothes that are ill-fitting and out of date, clothes that serve the purpose of clothing, but you would never be tempted to worship them. If necessary, go down to the thrift shop and get yourself something suitable. Remember that it has to be something you are a bit embarrassed to be seen in, or there's no point in doing this.
- If your cell phone is an idol, turn it off, and leave it off for a day. (You can keep it with you in case of emergency, but NO CHEATING. Leave it off unless you're calling 911.)
- If food is the idol, then go without for a day. If your health is delicate, talk with your doctor first.
- If your car is an idol, then do without it for a day. Take the bus, or walk. Or humble yourself enough to hitch a ride with someone. If you get help, give your driver gas money.
- If exercise is the idol, skip your workouts for a week. (Yes, I know, you'll start to lose your gains. In this case, that is the point. Spend the time praying for God to set your heart right about exercise and your body.)

After you have decided what idol you will fast from for a day, tell a friend to keep you each accountable. Ask each other throughout the day how it is going without your idol. List the idol and your accountability partner below.

Unit 9: The Divided Kingdom

2. Mock Your Idols. Psalm 115:3-8 gives a great example of idol-mockery, which is an excellent strategy to use to put an idol in its place. One way to mock an idol is to compare and contrast it with Jesus. Read Philippians 2:5-11 and use it to mock your idol. Fill in the blank of each question below with an idol that you struggle with.

Is _____ equal with God?

Did _____ give up equal glory with God and become human for you?

Did _____ obey the Father and die on the cross for you?

Has God exalted _____ and put it on His throne?

Will He make every knee bow to _____ in the end?

How did mocking your idol in this way change how you perceive your idol? _____

_____
_____
_____
_____
_____

Lesson 9.3

EVALUATION

1. What sort of king was Josiah at the beginning of his reign? _____
_____
_____

2. How could Josiah not know that worshiping Yahweh meant getting rid of all the idols? _____
_____
_____
_____

3. How did Israel lose the Bible? _____
_____
_____

4. What did Josiah do when he heard the book of the covenant? _____
_____
_____

5. What prophecy was fulfilled in Josiah's reign? _____
_____
_____
_____

6. How did God respond to Josiah's obedience?_____
_____
_____
_____

7. Why does Yahweh not share worship with idols? As long as people worship Him, what does He care if they worship something else on the side?_____
_____
_____

LESSON 9.4

Yahweh's Restoration of Judah

THE STORY

Lesson Theme - God kept His promise and returned Judah to the land after discipline.
This lesson is about God restoring Judah to the land after discipline. God is a loving Father, not a cosmic grinch. God kept His promise and returned His people to the land after He disciplined them. It's terribly important to end the Old Testament on this note: God may discipline, but He always restores us. He is not out to punish us, but to grow us into maturity.

Before we get started, a quick note on terminology. The word "Jew" comes from "Judah," and it was coined during the Babylonian captivity. During the divided kingdom period, the northern kingdom was known as Israel, and the southern kingdom was known as Judah, but the inhabitants of both kingdoms were still known as Israelites. When Babylon took the kingdom of Judah into captivity, all the captive people became known as Jews, and the term stuck when they came back home.

Before they had ever left Judah, God had discussed the exile with the prophet Habakkuk. Habakkuk had approached God and asked why He was not judging Judah's sin (Hab 1:2-4), and God explained that He was preparing the Babylonians (a.k.a. Chaldeans), "a bitter and hasty nation," to come and destroy Judah (Hab 1:5-11). Habakkuk objected that the Babylonians were even worse than Judah, and how could God allow that (Hab 1:12-2:1)? God answered him that the wicked Babylonians would be judged in their turn (Hab 2:5-20), but before giving that answer, God also

OVERVIEW

When He sent Judah into exile in Babylon, Yahweh promised that He would bring them back after 70 years, and He fulfilled His promise through a three-wave process. Zerubbabel brought back the first wave of people and rebuilt the temple. Ezra led the second wave of people, beautified the temple and brought reforms where the people had fallen into sin. Nehemiah led a third wave of restoration, rebuilding the wall and further reforming the spiritual life of the nation.

SOURCE MATERIAL

- 2 Chronicles 36:15-23
- Ezra
- Nehemiah
- Habakkuk
- Psalm 126
- Proverbs 21:1
- Psalms 137-150

made a promise: "Behold the proud, his soul is not upright in him, but the just shall live by his faith" (Hab 2:4). In context, this promise was that while the judgment was certainly coming, the people who trusted in God would be preserved through the judgment. Habakkuk responded to God's promise with one of the most beautiful songs of trust in the whole Bible, which can be found in Habakkuk 3.

Unit 9: The Divided Kingdom

OBJECTIVES

Feel...

- relief that God is true to His promises.
- happiness that God restored the nation of Israel after discipline.

Understand...

- that God was sending the people of Israel back to the land in fulfillment of His promise.
- that God didn't restore everything instantly. There was a process:
  * Zerubbabel brought the initial population and rebuilt the temple.
  * Ezra brought more people, beautified the temple, and brought much needed reform to the spiritual life of the people.
  * Nehemiah built the walls of Jerusalem, gave the people back their dignity, and continued the work of reform.
- that although the people still faced various problems in the land, they did *not* worship idols anymore—their captivity cured them of that problem, for good.
- that Nehemiah in particular was a man of faith and prayer; he prayed about *everything*.

Apply this understanding by...

- having an increased willingness to repent, knowing that God will restore you.
- following Nehemiah's example, praying for the same kinds of things as Nehemiah did and praying *constantly* like Nehemiah did.

God made good on His promise throughout the Babylonian captivity. When Shadrach, Meshach and Abed-nego were thrown into a furnace for refusing to bow down to the idol of the king, God miraculously preserved them from the flames. When Daniel dared to pray to God even though the king had decreed no one could pray to anyone but him, Daniel was thrown into the lions' den, but God closed the lions' mouths. When Haman secured a decree making it legal to kill all the Jews throughout the empire, God raised up Queen Esther to save them.

The first wave returned to Israel

God was faithful to His promises. God had also promised to send the Jews back home to the land. When the time had come for Judah to return home, Cyrus, king of Persia, gave the command that the Israelites should return and rebuild the temple at Jerusalem (2 Chr 36:23; Ezra 1:2). He returned the items Nebuchadnezzar had taken from the temple, and he commanded the Gentile people to be generous and send supplies for rebuilding the temple (Ezra 1:4-7). Along with the Gentiles' generosity in contributing materials for the construction of the temple, the Jews themselves contributed a great deal of gold, silver, and priestly garments. From wherever they had scattered throughout the empire over the last 70 years, they returned. Ezra reports that 42,360 free people went back to the land, taking with them 7,337 servants (Ezra 2).

They returned to their home cities and began to re-establish themselves under the leadership of Zerubbabel; then, in the seventh month, they went up to Jerusalem (Ezra 3:1). At this point the people had been in the land for a little while, and they had begun to fear the people around them (Ezra 3:3), but they proceeded anyway. They built the altar and began to make sacrifices on the first day of the seventh month; thereafter,

Israel and Judah's Exile

1. Assyrians took Israel into captivity (734–721 B.C.).
2. Babylonians took Judah into captivity (604–586 B.C.).
3. Judah returned from captivity to Jerusalem 70 years later.

Unit 9: The Divided Kingdom

they observed the morning and evening sacrifices, the new moons, and all the appointed feasts (Ezra 3:3-6). While there in Jerusalem, they also celebrated the Feast of Tabernacles, which was to be observed on the fifteenth day of the seventh month (Lev 23:34).

In the second month of the second year after they returned, the people gathered together again and laid the foundations of the temple (Ezra 3:8). Once the builders had laid the foundations, the priests and Levites praised God according to the musical service that David had initiated. Meanwhile, the people shouted for joy, but the old men who had seen the first temple (which had been destroyed 72 years earlier) wept (Ezra 3:10-12).

The Israelites, however, experienced opposition to the rebuilding of the temple. The Israelites were already afraid of the other people in the land by the time they built the altar. Now that work had begun on the temple, resistance intensified. The Samaritans came up and asked to be made partners in the building. On the surface, their request seems like it was a friendly offer, but Ezra describes them as "adversaries" from the outset (Ezra 4:1). The Samaritans said that they had been serving Yahweh since they first came into the land under the Assyrians. While this was true, they also worshiped idols alongside Yahweh (see 2 Kgs 17:24-41). Idol worship was the kind of trouble that got Israel sent into exile to start with, and Israel was taking no chances on getting into that kind of trouble again. They declined the Samaritans' help (Ezra 4:3), and drew legal support for their decision from Cyrus' decree, which said the Israelites should be the ones to rebuild the temple.

It's hard to weigh the Jews' decision here. On one hand, the Samaritans were impure in their worship, and there was a real risk there. On the other hand, God's plan for Israel was always for them to be a light to the nations. The Jews could have said, "We'd love to have you join us, but if you want to help, you have to forsake all your other gods." Instead, they simply rejected the Samaritans out of hand. As a result, the Samaritans hired lobbyists to make trouble at court for Israel, from the days of Cyrus right on into the reign of Darius and even into the reign of Artaxerxes.

(Ezra 4:6-23 is a parenthesis. The chronological flow continues up to Ezra 4:5 and then resumes in Ezra 4:24. Ezra 4:6-23 is an excursus on Samaritan opposition at court and skip ahead through the reign of a number of kings. The opposition was apparently most successful under Artaxerxes, but it was also under his reign that the wall was completed, so evidently the opponents didn't succeed for very long.)

Because the Samaritans had discouraged them in various ways, construction was stalled until the second year of King Darius (Ezra 4:25), when the prophetic ministries of Haggai and Zechariah inspired the people to begin building the temple again (Ezra 5:1). The governor of the province, Tattenai, not knowing of Cyrus' original decree authorizing the work, tried to make the Jews stop building the temple. But the Jews told Tattenai of Cyrus' decree and continued doing the work (Ezra 5:5). Tattenai wrote to Darius to find out if the people were telling him the truth, and Darius had the archives searched (Ezra 6:1). They discovered Cyrus' original decree, and Darius not only confirmed it, but added that if anyone altered his edict, a timber should be pulled from that man's house and erected, the man hanged from it, and his house made a refuse heap (Ezra 6:11). Suddenly the Jews had all the support they needed: the empire paid the expenses, supplied the building materials, and even supplied everything for the sacrifices, in order that the Jews would pray for the life of the king and his sons (Ezra 6:8-10). The Jews completed the work four years later and celebrated the Passover again in a completed temple.

Some years went by. The walls of Jerusalem were still in ruins, leaving the Jewish people terribly vulnerable to raids from Samaritans and other enemies. But the temple was completed and functioning, and the people were living in the land and worshiping Yahweh again.

Ezra's reforms
In 458 B.C., Ezra the scribe brought another wave of returning Jews to the land (Ezra 7:1-7). Ezra came with a decree from Artaxerxes I installing him as governor with a charter to beautify the temple and enforce both the Law of Yahweh and the law of the king in the land (Ezra 7:11-26). To Ezra's great consternation, he found the people had already violated the Law of Yahweh by intermarrying again with the peoples of the land; the practice was so pervasive that even many of the priests had taken pagan wives (Ezra 9:1-3).

Ezra commanded all the Jews to appear in Jerusalem and called out their sin; and they repented. However, because there were so many of them, they had to come back in groups to deal with the problem a few at a time. In the end, the men put away their pagan wives and again served the Lord faithfully (Ezra 9-10).

Nehemiah's reforms
During all this time, there were still many Jews remaining in exile. Some of them were in prominent government positions and unable to leave (e.g., Daniel), while others apparently simply chose to stay. Nehemiah was one of those with a high position; he was cupbearer to King Artaxerxes. The cupbearer was the one who brought the king his wine and tasted it ahead of him to be sure it wasn't poisoned; it was a position of extreme responsibility and trust.

Word came to Nehemiah that Jerusalem was still in ruins and the returned exiles were discouraged and afraid. Notice the first thing he did was pray (Neh 1:4-11). It was only after he prayed that God opened the way for him to do anything else.

One of the privileges of being king is that you can insist that anyone in your presence should put on a happy face for your benefit—after all, it's a joy to serve the king, right? So in all his time as the king's cupbearer, Nehemiah had never been sad before him (Neh 2:1). But after word came to Nehemiah that Jerusalem was still in ruins, he was unable to even pretend to be happy. The king asked what was wrong, and Nehemiah was afraid, because he knew he could be executed for even coming into the king's presence sad (Neh 2:2). But he answered honestly, and the king asked him what he wanted. Again, Nehemiah prayed before proceeding, then asked for permission to go to Judah for a limited time and rebuild the city (Neh 2:4-5).

The king agreed and issued the necessary orders for Nehemiah's passage and supplies (Neh 2:6), and immediately the enemies of the Jews were troubled (Neh 2:10). (Remember, the Jews' enemies in the land were paying for lobbyists to bad-mouth the Jews at court. They may well have had word of the king's decree even before Nehemiah arrived). Upon his arrival, Nehemiah told no one his business, but went out at night and surveyed the city walls, which were damaged extensively (Neh 2:12).

Only after he had completed his survey did Nehemiah announce to the Jews what he intended to do and that he had the king's blessing (Neh 2:17-18). The people came willingly to work,

Unit 9: The Divided Kingdom

each family taking responsibility for a different portion of the wall. However, the Samaritans and the Gentiles in the land mocked and discouraged them (Neh 2:19, 4:1).

When mocking didn't stop the rebuilding work, Judah's enemies conspired together to attack the city (Neh 4:8). Nehemiah heard of it and stationed warriors at strategic places along the wall. In addition, he instructed each of the workers to strap on his sword, hold a weapon in one hand and do the construction work with the other. Still, the workers were dispersed all along the wall, so he instructed the people to blow a trumpet if they were attacked, and everyone would rally to the trumpet. The people were undaunted, and the work continued (Neh 4:9-23). Seeing that their plot was known, the enemies of the Jews did not attack.

However, trouble continued, both internally and externally. Internally, the Jewish nobles were oppressing their poorer brothers. Nehemiah rebuked them by pointing out that they had redeemed their enslaved brothers from all the Gentile lands where they were scattered, but now they were enslaving those very people to their own Jewish brothers. They all repented (Neh 5:1-13).

Externally, the enemies of the Jews, having failed in a direct attack on the city, now tried several times to lure Nehemiah into an assassination trap, but he refused to meet them each time (Neh 6). At length, the wall was completed, and the enemies were greatly discouraged.

With the wall rebuilt, Judah was still under the empire of Persia, but they now had a capital city again, and the nation's dignity was restored. Life in the land could begin in earnest. When the people came together again to observe the Feast of Tabernacles (Neh 8), Ezra read the Law of Moses to the people, and they began to mourn, realizing that the way they were living was displeasing to God. The leaders told the people not to mourn, because the Feast of Tabernacles was a joyful feast; mourning was not appropriate (Neh 8:9). (The leaders were right about this; Tabernacles was like a week-long Thanksgiving feast where the people were required to spend 10% of their annual income on the party. God did not want them mourning during this time.) So they continued with the feast, but Ezra read to the people from the Law every day, and they all took an oath to keep the entire Law (Neh 9-10).

Nehemiah also gathered the musicians and had them perform worship to dedicate the newly constructed walls of Jerusalem and then to continue ministering in the temple (Neh 12:7). The whole nation gave to provide for the musicians' needs so they could give themselves continually to worship in the temple.

However, everything wasn't perfect, as we see in Nehemiah 13. Nehemiah had to return to the king of Persia as he had originally agreed (see Neh 2:6), and when he came back again to Jerusalem, he found that some problems had cropped up with the temple worship, Sabbath observance, and intermarriage with pagans. He insisted (again!) on reform, and he got it. At this point, the historical books leave the story: Yahweh had restored the nation to the land after disciplining them. They no longer worshiped idols—which was the sin He had been disciplining them for. They were still a long way from perfect, and they were still falling into different sorts of sin. But they were improving, and they responded well when someone pointed out their sin—which was a *major* improvement over the way they had responded to the prophets before the exile.

APPLICATION

Judah is a lot like us. Even when we really do learn a solid lesson (as Judah did about not worshiping idols), we still have plenty of room for growth. But if we respond well to correction, there's hope, just like there was for Judah.

Part of responding well is praying, and we need to follow Nehemiah's example of prayer. Notice that he prayed constantly and that he also confessed the sins of his people, not just his own personal sins. This is hard for modern people to grasp; we tend to want to say, "I'm not doing that stuff, so why should I confess it?" Nehemiah did not have that perspective, nor should we. Spend some time confessing the sins of your people to God and asking Him to have mercy and bring repentance.

ACTIVITIES

1. Praying like Nehemiah: Praying for Your People. Read Nehemiah's prayer in Nehemiah 1. Nehemiah was a righteous man, but he didn't say, "I don't have anything to do with all these sins that other Jews are committing." Instead, he took responsibility saying, "We have acted very corruptly...." (Neh 1:7). Nehemiah confessed the sins of his society. Draft a prayer below in which you pray for our society the same way Nehemiah prayed for his: confess the sins of the nation, review the history of what God has done for us, and ask for His blessing.

Unit 9: The Divided Kingdom

2. Praying like Nehemiah: Praying Constantly. Read through the book of Nehemiah and mark every place where Nehemiah prayed. Answer the questions below about Nehemiah's prayers.

On what occasions did Nehemiah typically pray? _____

_____
_____
_____
_____
_____
_____
_____
_____

What did Nehemiah pray about? _____

_____
_____
_____
_____
_____
_____
_____

What can you learn from Nehemiah's prayers? _____

_____
_____
_____
_____
_____
_____
_____

EVALUATION

1. Why did God bring Judah back into the land? _____

_____

2. Did God restore everything instantly for Judah? _____

3. What were the three waves of God's restoration of Judah to the land, and who led each wave? ____

_____

_____

_____

4. The city wall was a basic necessity for self-defense. Why did the people of Judah build the temple first and then the city wall afterward? _____

_____

5. What sort of resistance did the returning exiles have to deal with? _____

_____

_____

6. Now that they had been disciplined by God and restored to the land as He had promised, the people walked with God and didn't have any more major problems with sin...right? _____

_____

7. But what one sin did they *not* fall into again?_____

_____

8. Weren't they nearly as bad off as before, if they were continuing to fall into all these other sins?____

_____

_____

_____

_____

_____